Let Love S[...]

Reflections on Renewal i[...]

Bishop Donal Murray lectured in Mor[...]
and in Holy Cross College from 1969 [...]
of Dublin from 1982 to 1996 and then Bishop of Limerick until [...]
He is now retired.

BISHOP DONAL MURRAY

LET LOVE SPEAK

Reflections on Renewal
in the Irish Church

VERITAS

Published 2011 by
Veritas Publications
7–8 Lower Abbey Street
Dublin 1
Ireland

publications@veritas.ie
www.veritas.ie

ISBN 978-1-84730-268-7

Designed by Lir Mac Cárthaigh, Veritas
Printed in the Republic of Ireland by Hudson Killeen, Dublin

*Veritas books are printed on paper made from the wood pulp of managed forests. For every
tree felled, at least one tree is planted, thereby renewing natural resources.*

CONTENTS

INTRODUCTION   7

CHAPTER ONE:
The Promise Slips Away   10

CHAPTER TWO:
All Our Perfectness   23

CHAPTER THREE:
God's Most Stupendous Attribute   36

CHAPTER FOUR:
The Sleeping Giant   50

CHAPTER FIVE:
Not Power But Love   65

CHAPTER SIX:
Morality in Crisis   81

CHAPTER SEVEN:
Built into a Spiritual House   101

CHAPTER EIGHT:
The Triumph of Mr Gradgrind?   118

CHAPTER NINE:
Pray Without Ceasing   135

CHAPTER TEN:
Communion With Christ and With One Another   153

'God is love, and he who abides in love abides in God, and God abides in him' (1 Jn 4:16). These words from the First Letter of John express with remarkable clarity the heart of the Christian faith: the Christian image of God and the resulting image of mankind and its destiny. In the same verse, Saint John also offers a kind of summary of the Christian life: 'We have come to know and to believe in the love God has for us.'[1]

The opening words of Pope Benedict's first encyclical focus on the essentials – 'the heart of the Christian faith' and 'a kind of summary of the Christian life'. The Pope goes on to say that this verse of St John's First Epistle also expresses 'the fundamental decision' of the life of a Christian.

In the crisis that we in Ireland are experiencing, in Church, in State, in many institutions and areas of society, it would be easy to feel swamped and disheartened. The reflections in this book do not attempt the impossible task of examining all the dimensions of the issues that need to be addressed. They seek to look at a number of aspects of a changing Ireland in the light of the central truth about God who is love and whose Word took flesh and lived among us. That central truth is also the source of the 'wonder and

---

1. Benedict XVI, *Deus caritas est*, 1; all Vatican documents cited throughout can be accessed through www.vatican.va.

amazement'[2] with which we see ourselves in the light of the Incarnation of God's Word and our redemption in Christ.

We can find meaning and inspiration in the heart of Christian faith. We need to try to see our various crises and challenges in the light of the Good News that 'God so loved the world that he gave his only Son, that whoever believes in him should have eternal life' (Jn 3:16).[3]

I am convinced that it is here, with these fundamental truths, in our encounter with the Word made flesh, that renewal has to start. In that encounter we will find the deepest reasons for hope, and the most uncomfortable challenges to our half-heartedness, our complacency, our rationalisations and our failures to recognise and live the truth. It is there, too, that the Church in Ireland will find the courage and the creativity to respond to the call of Pope John Paul II in Knock to look constantly 'for new ways that will enable her to understand more profoundly and to carry out with renewed vigour the mission received from her Founder'.

Pope Benedict clearly presents this as the path to renewal in Ireland now:

> In confronting the present crisis, measures to deal justly with individual crimes are essential, yet on their own they are not enough: a new vision is needed, to inspire present and future generations to treasure the gift of our common faith. By treading the path marked out by the Gospel, by observing the commandments and by conforming your lives more closely to the figure of Jesus Christ, you will surely experience the profound renewal that is so urgently needed at this time.[4]

The fruit of that vision will make many demands in all of the areas looked at in this book — in the participation of everybody in the

---

2. John Paul II, *Redemptor hominis*, 10.
3. All Scripture is taken from the *Revised Standard Version Bible*, unless otherwise stated.
4. Benedict XVI, *Pastoral Letter to the Catholics of Ireland*, 12.

life and mission of the Church, in areas such as education at every level, in social and political life. The need to 'fix things', the quest for perfect structures is not the first step. It is vital that the efforts we make should be founded on that vision and on our seeking to grow closer to Christ. The changes that this will require of us will be no less radical for that; they will set us on the path to a renewal which leaves no room for complacency. We will know that we are part of the unending race described by St Paul:

> Not that I have already obtained this or am already perfect; but I press on to make it my own, because Christ Jesus has made me his own. Brethren, I do not consider that I have made it my own; but one thing I do, forgetting what lies behind and straining forward to what lies ahead, I press on toward the goal for the prize of the upward call of God in Christ Jesus. (Phil 3:12-14)

CHAPTER ONE

The Promise Slips Away

Who would have thought my shrivel'd heart
could have recover'd greenness? It was gone
quite under ground; as flowers depart
to see their mother-root, when they have blown;
where they together
all the hard weather,
dead to the world, keep house unknown.

These are Thy wonders, Lord of power,
killing and quickening, bringing down to hell
and up to heaven in an hour;
making a chiming of a passing-bell.
We say amiss
this or that is:
Thy word is all, if we could spell. [...]

These are Thy wonders, Lord of love,
to make us see we are but flowers that glide;
which when we once can finde and prove,
Thou hast a garden for us where to bide.
Who would be more,
swelling through store,
forfeit their paradise by their pride.[1]

---

1. George Herbert (1595–1633), extract from 'The Flower': http://www.ccel.org/h/
herbert/temple/ Flower.html [accessed 12 February 2011]. See *The Divine Office I*
(Dublin: Talbot Press, 1974), p. 578.

Twenty-five years ago Robert Bellah and a number of colleagues felt the need to examine modern society from the perspective of social science, while keeping the boundary to philosophy 'still open'. In other words, they wished to look not just at what was happening but at its meaning. They raised a question that resonates today:

> There is a widespread feeling that the promise of the modern era is slipping away from us. A movement of enlightenment and liberation that was to have freed us from superstition and tyranny has led in the twentieth century to a world in which ideological fanaticism and political oppression have reached extremes unknown in previous history.[2]

A quarter of a century later, it might be more correct to say that there is a widespread feeling that the *promise has already slipped away*. There seems to be an ever-present sense of powerlessness and anger about many things in our society. Unquestioned assumptions of continually growing affluence have evaporated. For some among us, of course, such expectations always seemed distant, receding and alienating, merely highlighting their sense of exclusion.

For most of us, it seems only recently that we celebrated the arrival of the new millennium. Ireland had, to its own surprise, entered a period of unimagined prosperity that seemed likely to last indefinitely. We had hopes, even expectations, that the twenty-first century would offer an era of peace and prosperity. We could begin to glimpse the prospect of progress and fairness unmatched in human history.

Instead, the first decade of this century brought more, much more, of the same: terrorism, war, natural disaster and economic collapse. The Celtic Tiger, which seemed so full of vigour and new

---

2. Robert N. Bellah et al., *Habits of the Heart* (Berkeley: University of California Press, 1985), p. 277.

possibilities, is dead. We wonder if we are a better society for the experience and whether the promise was real at all. There is a weakening of the hope and of the solidarity which every society needs if it is to thrive, or even survive.

Well-Founded Disenchantment

Banks, developers and politicians have questions to answer about the greed and foolishness that were at the root of the financial collapse. Many of the rest of us have to ask whether we were too ready to believe that our country was about to be rich beyond imagining. And we hear the voices that ask how, during a time when the State was 'awash with money', so many remained at the margins with inadequate incomes and housing, and with little reason to hope that they would ever have a share in that wealth.

All of the many people who experienced sexual and physical abuse as children suffered a serious assault on their personal dignity and rights, an attack on their sense of their own worth and an undermining of their ability to trust themselves, to trust other people and sometimes even to trust God. The abuser has often left them a most cruel legacy: a persistent feeling – which has no foundation in objective reality – that they are to blame for what occurred. The abuse was inflicted by an adult on a helpless child. No blame at all can be attributed to the child.

Survivors are entitled to a readiness to listen to their painful accounts and a recognition of the evil and horror that they were forced to suffer and of the betrayal that was involved. They should be able to feel fully supported on the road towards rebuilding their lives and their serenity. This is not an issue that can be dealt with by particular agencies alone. The Gardaí, the Health Service Executive, the Church, have important responsibilities; retribution and the payment of compensation by those responsible also have a place. But if this hurt is to be healed, it requires that the survivor experience respect and regard in the community as a whole. They should also know that as far as possible, people are willing to try to understand their often long and painful journey towards healing. They are entitled to feel supported in the many different kinds of restoration they need in their lives, such as the rediscovery of an ability to relate with trust for others, the repairing of what were often lost years of education, the rebuilding of relationships that were made more difficult by the scars of abuse.

The privacy of the survivor must be respected, but we must not think that any part of society can simply regard it as someone else's task to respond to the horror that has taken place within it. In particular, the whole community needs to be aware of the scale of this pain. The figures show that the issue is on a far greater scale than our society has yet been willing to face. Even today, the findings of the SAVI Report (2002) are incredulously denied or studiously ignored. Many find it impossible to believe that more than one child in five could have been sexually abused before the age of seventeen.[3]

The Church, the whole of society and each one of us have to ask ourselves how this terror could have been inflicted on little children, why we failed to recognise what was happening and how we can best work to prevent it happening again. Each of us needs to recognise how the instinctive reaction that 'this cannot be true' can blind us. Until we realise in painful reality how difficult it is to believe that a person we have known and trusted has molested a child, we will not be able to face the truth. Perhaps that lesson can only be learned in excruciating experience.

The young look at the massive debts and problems that we are leaving to them and perhaps to their children's children. They look to a future that is full of widely varying threats: violent crime, uncontrollable terror, the disintegration of society, rampant individualism, climate change, unemployment and financial turmoil, increasingly chaotic moral discourse, the reign of tyranny, and the shortage not just of oil but of absolutely vital necessities

---

3. See Hannah McGee et al., *The SAVI Report: Sexual Abuse and Violence in Ireland* (Dublin: The Liffey Press in association with the Dublin Rape Crisis Centre, 2002), pp. xxxiif and chap. 4, pp. 55–186.

like water. The reaction to all of this, in private conversations, in pub-talk, on social networks or in the traditional media, risks feeding our disillusionment while failing to point to any way forward. In the context of these threats, we need to ask whether we can find a promise that will not slip away as did the earlier promise.

It is easy to say that suffering and shortage will be good for us. It may in some ways turn out to be so, depending on how we respond to it. But it would be wrong to suggest that a decent standard of living, a degree of affluence, a good education or the means to tackle social problems at home and abroad are harmful in themselves. What is bad is that in the past we failed to use such opportunities responsibly and generously in a way that would have made our present world more just, more human and more able to respond to the crisis.

We now need an effort to build our society on something more solid, more true, more humanly valuable than the deceptive promises of the Celtic Tiger. We need to ask serious questions about where we are going and why. The purpose of our life as a community must be something more than the acquisition of wealth and property. We need to look critically at the assumptions that led us to where we are.

We should not complacently assume that people of other cultures — some with traditions every bit as ancient and rich as our own — look on an affluent Western lifestyle with undiluted envy and longing. There would be an obvious flaw in any such aspiration. The goal of sharing the affluent Western way of life with the whole human family, at least with our present resources, or any imaginable future means and technologies, is an unattainable dream. It would require a hugely accelerated consumption of the earth's diminishing resources. In any case, there was little enough sign of our widespread affluence being shared with the rest of the world, or even with sections of our own population.

Even apart from that, there are many people in the world who question whether a society which seems to have so little time and space for the really important things – family, community, religion, friendship – is really as 'advanced' as it imagines.

We need to see in the challenge of today – as we should have seen in the opportunities of yesterday – the questions that remain always fundamental but are often ignored. Why are we here? Has human life a meaning? How does our attitude to that question affect how we live in society? How does it affect the goals that we set as individuals, as groups, as a community, as the human family? Can we make any effective impact on the vast needs of the developing world? Does our concern have any effect other than making ourselves feel guilty? Is the ideal of a just and fully human society an illusion? Why does nothing ever fully satisfy us? How can we begin to find truth and a sense of direction in the midst of so many conflicting views, even on basic moral issues? How can life make sense in the light of the terrible suffering that people endure? Are human efforts and human achievements always destined to crumble? What happens when we die? What has happened to the dead relatives and friends whom we love and miss?

Unlimited Hopes

Serious reflection on such questions reveals our vulnerability, our sense of powerlessness in the face of economic, political, moral and social failures in ourselves and in those around us. We are aware that although we can and must try to alleviate all of this suffering, we will never eliminate it. A realistic acknowledgement of our inability to resolve all the problems is a good place to start.

Those failures and the disillusionment they breed can lead us to see that our sense of helplessness arises precisely because our hopes are unlimited. We long for peace, for justice, for truth, for fulfilment; but we never find them except in an impermanent, fragile, imperfect form. Nothing we have experienced or will experience in our lives is the final goal that would satisfy us and all humanity. Nothing we build is perfect; our efforts to repair injuries that we have inflicted always fall short; our closest relationships are fragile; our hopes are never completely fulfilled. The injustices that all of us have suffered, and some people have suffered in horrific ways, may be healed only very slowly and never completely. Every person, including ourselves, will die.

It is there, in our deepest longing, that we may hear the still, small voice of God (cf. 1 Kings 19:12). That was what the Second Vatican Council said: 'When [people] are drawn to think about their real selves they turn to those deep recesses of their being where God who probes the heart awaits them and where they themselves decide their own destiny in the sight of God.'[4]

That is where the search for hope has to begin. It cannot start in fantasies or unrealistic dreams or in a goal which would not permanently satisfy us even if we could achieve it. The journey must start from where we are, with all the darkness and sorrow that often comes upon us and with our fears and vulnerability about the fragile nature of even our most wonderful joys and our deepest relationships. We are creatures who seek a beauty that will not pass. We cannot even imagine what it would be like to be in untroubled contemplation of infinite beauty and truth and joy, sharing that joy with the whole human family. Threats from ourselves or from others, from within our relationships or from outside: violence, dishonesty, jealousy, illness, separation, financial ruin, infidelity and death loom over everything that means most to us.

If there is a goal for human life that will fully satisfy us, it has to be not just a benign force or a power, but a Being who is the source of unlimited, unassailable, unending life and love. If we are to have a hope that would satisfy, it would have to be a hope that can look death and evil and suffering and failure in the face and can find even in that darkness, perhaps especially in that darkness, the light that darkness is not able to overcome (cf. Jn 1:5).

On the day of his Inauguration, Pope Benedict looked towards the various terrible situations in which people live their lives:

---

4. Second Vatican Council, *Gaudium et spes*, 14.

[T]here are so many kinds of desert. There is the desert of poverty, the desert of hunger and thirst, the desert of abandonment, of loneliness, of destroyed love. There is the desert of God's darkness, the emptiness of souls no longer aware of their dignity or the goal of human life. The external deserts in the world are growing, because the internal deserts have become so vast.[5]

The depth of these experiences is increased in our time because our situation discourages any search that explores more deeply than our culture feels comfortable going. Religious questions, which have to do with the meaning of life and death, the possibility of forgiveness, the source of a hope large enough to satisfy us, 'the goal of human life', are presented as if they were, at best, private answers to private questions. The truth is that they are the fundamental questions about who we are and what our lives, including our lives in society, mean.

The promise that is heard in the voice of God is not just a new version of our hopes at the beginning of the new millennium; it is the fulfilling of all human hopes – yours and mine, the first human beings, those who have lived in civilisations vastly different from our own, the people who were alive at the dawn of human history, the first artist who painted animals on the walls of caves, and the artists who will work in new styles and new materials, as yet undiscovered, the scientists who will unlock secrets about creation that we have not yet imagined, the astronaut explorers who will visit other worlds. And in that fulfilment everyone will share in and rejoice in everyone else's gifts as much as they do in their own,[6] because they will see in each person a unique reflection of the Creator who is the Father of all. We will be with Christ at his Father's side; we will see our goal and understand the real meaning of fulfilment:

---

5. Benedict XVI, Homily at Mass for the Inauguration of his Pontificate, 24 April 2005.
6. See Aquinas, *Commentary on the Creed*, 12: http://dhspriory.org/thomas/Creed.htm#12 [accessed 12 February 2011].

The Lord is the goal of human history, the focal point of the desires of history and of civilisation, the centre of humanity, the joy of all hearts, and the fulfilment of all aspirations.[7]

Recapturing the Vision

Our immediate response when we are asked how we can renew the Church in the darkness that we see around us is to think in terms of the tasks that need to be done and the structures that need to be changed or perhaps demolished.

All of those questions have their importance, and we will touch on some of them in this book, but they are not the foundations on which the Church is built or rebuilt. Pope John Paul was insistent that all renewal begins in what the Second Vatican Council termed 'the universal call to holiness'.[8] That call is for everyone. Baptism is 'the true entry into the holiness of God' and so

> [...] it would be a contradiction to settle for a life of mediocrity [...]
> To ask catechumens: 'Do you wish to receive Baptism?' means at the same time to ask them: 'Do you wish to be holy?' It means to set before them the radical nature of the Sermon on the Mount: 'Be perfect as your heavenly Father is perfect.' (Mt 5:48)[9]

Jesus was not pointing to a short cut, a gentle stroll, but to a demanding journey on a road that leads to the Cross. Being a Christian is not meant to be easy: 'Whoever does not take up the cross and follow me is not worthy of me' (Mt 10:38; *New Revised Standard Version Bible*). Any suggestion that there is an undemanding way for any of us – laity, religious, or ordained ministers – to play our part in the renewal of the Church is a destructive illusion.

Pope John Paul told us in Limerick that there was no such thing as an ordinary layperson: 'All of you have been called to conversion

---

7. *Gaudium et spes*, 45.
8. See Second Vatican Council, *Lumen gentium*, chap. 5, 39–42.
9. John Paul II, *Novo millennio ineunte*, 30, 31.

through the death and resurrection of Jesus Christ. As God's holy people you are called to fulfil your role in the evangelisation of the world.'[10]

So a reflection on how the Church in Ireland is to be renewed has to begin by asking what it means to be perfect as the Father is perfect. We need to ask how all of us, lay, ordained and religious, young and old, can reawaken and breathe new life into our commitment to the task of growing in holiness. We need to ask how we can grow in the understanding of his Way as the only path to the goal that is offered to us. We need to ask how we can see our own personal and social contexts in the light and challenge of the Good News. We need to ask ourselves how we can carry out more fully the mission that is given to each one and to all of us together.[11]

Only if we can recapture that vision will we begin to understand what the Church is about and will we begin to see what is required in order to renew its life in our hearts and in our society:

> Although the Church possesses a 'hierarchical' structure, nevertheless this structure is totally ordered to the holiness of Christ's members. And holiness is measured according to the 'great mystery' in which the Bride responds with the gift of love to the gift of the Bridegroom. She does this 'in the Holy Spirit', since 'God's love has been poured into our hearts through the Holy Spirit who has been given to us'. (Rom 5:5)[12]

Something similar is true of society, which has a structure called the State. Like all structures, the Church included, the State is in constant danger of seeing itself as an entity existing for its own benefit. The role of the State is to promote the conditions which

---

10. John Paul II, Homily in Limerick, 1 October 1979.

11. John Paul II, Homily in Knock, 30 September 1979.

12. John Paul II, *Mulieris dignitatem*, 27.

allow people as groups and as individuals to flourish and be fulfilled: 'It is the role of the state to defend and promote the common good of civil society, its citizens and intermediate bodies.'[13]

In both cases there is a danger of reducing our understanding of reality in a way that loses sight of the meaning and purpose of the structures which any community needs. This can result in attempts to reform the structures without any reference to their purpose. The structures of the State exist for certain limited purposes which are to be achieved by political and economic policies, legislation, law enforcement, taxation and so on. This has to do with particular aspects of our lives but not the whole of ourselves. There are aspects of life – people's private opinions and their friendships, for instance – which are no concern of the State unless they impinge on the rest of the community or the common good.

The structures of the Church also exist for a specific purpose. They exist in order to serve the purpose for which the Church exists, namely to draw us closer to Christ and one another, and to enable all members of the Church to respond with the gift of their lives to him:

> This is of fundamental importance for understanding the Church in her own essence, so as to avoid applying to the Church – even in her dimension as an 'institution' made up of human beings and forming part of history – criteria of understanding and judgement which do not pertain to her nature. Although the Church possesses a 'hierarchical' structure, nevertheless *this structure is totally ordered to the holiness of Christ's members.*[14]

This is a statement about what the Church is meant to be. It is, in other words, the criterion for assessing how true the structure is

---

13. *Catechism of the Catholic Church* (Dublin: Veritas, 1994), 1910.
14. *Mulieris dignitatem*, 27 (my italics).

to the purpose for which it exists. It is the criterion for genuine renewal.

The task that faces us is not simply one of 'putting Humpty Dumpty together again'. We in Europe, both in cultural and religious terms, live in a world in transition. Both the European culture we have taken for granted and the Gospel by which we try to live may, not for the first time, have to take root in a new situation. As Desmond Fennell put it, in a stimulating article:

> Ultimately, for one reason or another, the continuous increase of the collective and individual power to buy and do [...] will cease. And its vaunted moral superiority over all previous or existing lives will become an irrelevant twaddle. Nothing will then remain to prevent the direct and continuous impact of the system's senselessness on the consciousness of westerners, young and old, or to make that senseless and unloved life framework seem a good life.[15]

The promise of the Gospel does not slip away or die but there is a constant challenge to bring the Good News to new moments in history:

> Every generation, with its own mentality and characteristics, is like a new continent to be won for Christ. The Church must constantly look for new ways that will enable her to understand more profoundly and to carry out with renewed vigour the mission received from her Founder.[16]

---

15. Desmond Fennell, *Ireland After the End of Western Civilisation* (Cork: Athol Books, 2009), p. 24.
16. Homily in Knock, 30 September 1979.

Pope Benedict's Prayer for the Church of Ireland

God of our fathers,
renew us in the faith which is our life and salvation,
the hope which promises forgiveness and interior renewal,
the charity which purifies and opens our hearts
to love you, and in you, each of our brothers and sisters.

Lord Jesus Christ,
may the Church in Ireland renew her age-old commitment
to the education of our young people in the way of truth and
    goodness,
holiness and generous service to society.

Holy Spirit, comforter, advocate and guide,
inspire a new springtime of holiness and apostolic zeal
for the Church in Ireland.

May our sorrow and our tears,
our sincere effort to redress past wrongs,
and our firm purpose of amendment
bear an abundant harvest of grace
for the deepening of the faith
in our families, parishes, schools and communities,
for the spiritual progress of Irish society,
and the growth of charity, justice, joy and peace
within the whole human family.

To you, Triune God,
confident in the loving protection of Mary,
Queen of Ireland, our Mother,
and of St Patrick, St Brigid and all the saints,
do we entrust ourselves, our children,
and the needs of the Church in Ireland.
Amen.[17]

---

17. http://www.vatican.va/holy__father/benedict__xvi/letters/2010/documents/hf__
ben-xvi__let__20100319__church-ireland__en.html [accessed 12 February 2011].

CHAPTER TWO

All Our Perfectness

Who shall allot the praise, and guess
    What part is yours and what is ours? —
O years that certainly will bless
    Our flowers with fruits, our seeds with flowers,
With ruin all our perfectness.[1]

Precarious Joy

When we are weary and disheartened, or overcome in the sadness
and disillusionment of some terrible event, we cannot escape
fundamental questions about life and faith. 'I am heartbroken. I
cannot bear this feeling that everything is falling apart. Why
should this be happening to me? I've prayed as I never prayed
before; nothing is impossible for God; why would he not do this
one thing for me?'

This sense of loss and confusion is not because life is endlessly
miserable. It is because life can be so full of promise and joy and
love. But our joy is precarious. Often we are sad because we had
wonderful hopes which we now fear will be dashed, or because a
wonderful marriage or a much-valued friendship faces the
imminent separation of death. As we grow older, members of our

---

1. Alice Meynell, extract from 'Builders of Ruins', *The Poems of Alice Meynell, Complete
Edition* (1923): http://poetry.elcore.net/CatholicPoets/Meynell/Meynell010.html
[accessed 12 February 2011].

family and our friends suffer; they endure crises; they die. We become more aware that this is a 'beauty that will pass'.[2] The building of a beauty which would be perfect and endless is beyond us. Life cannot give us all that we hope for. If by some miracle we got everything we ever wanted, a lot of other people might be less than happy!

The Sermon on the Mount turns expectations upside down. It tells us that the meek, the mourners and the persecuted are blessed. When we are in a situation of pain and loss it often doesn't feel like that. Yet the very foundations of Christian faith lie in the shattered expectations of Good Friday.

Jesus suffered agony in the Garden of Gethsemane, with his most trusted friends failing to stay awake with him. He sweated blood and begged his Father that the cup of suffering might pass him by (Mt 26:39). He hung forsaken, mocked and agonised on the cross. Dying with Jesus is the beginning of a new life that lies beyond all pain and loss. The thought of rising to a new life beyond death and sorrow does not ease our pain. However much we reflect and pray, we may remain distraught and lost.

A Change of Outlook

The disciples who met the stranger on the road to Emmaus were grappling with disaster. They were walking along, 'looking sad' (Lk 24:17). They told the stranger how powerful the words and deeds of Jesus had been. They had hoped that he was the one to set Israel free; but now he had suffered the agonising, humiliating death of a common criminal. They were shattered. They had thought that Jesus would restore Israel to its former glory and fulfil the promises of God. Their hope was gone.

As they came to the end of their tale of lost hopes, they made a very interesting statement, a statement often overlooked when the Gospel account is read:

---

2. Padraic Pearse, 'The Wayfarer', in *Plays, Stories, Poems* (Dublin: Talbot Press, 1966), p. 341.

Some women of our group astounded us. They were at the tomb early this morning, and when they did not find his body there, they came back and told us that they had indeed seen a vision of angels, who said that he was alive. Some of those who were with us went to the tomb and found it just as the women had said; but they did not see him. (Lk 24:22-24; NRSV)

In other words, *the two disciples had already heard the Good News* but it had not lifted their gloom. That seems surprising, until we realise how well it describes our own situation. We have heard the Good News, but there are times when we feel downhearted and broken, as if our lives had lost all meaning. It is one thing to know the truth in the abstract; it is another to live it in the anguish of our ruined hopes. We often grieve like those who have no hope (cf. 1 Thess 4:13).

The disciples on the road were in turmoil; the story that Jesus had risen seemed just another source of confusion, another element of absurdity. To grasp what had happened would demand a change of outlook that would turn everything upside down, a change that they were quite unable to imagine, still less accept.

But that is what Jesus calls for; it marks all of his preaching – to see everything in a completely new way. There can be no renewal of the Church which does not take this call seriously: 'From that time, Jesus began to proclaim, "*Repent*, for the kingdom of heaven is at hand"' (Mt 4:17; my emphasis). Repentance or conversion, overturning our assumptions, is required of those who want to be part of the kingdom of God. The change of outlook we are called to is every bit as disconcerting, as unimaginable, as the change that was demanded of the two disciples. Every effort to follow Christ, including any effort to renew the Church and to look to the challenges that face us, begins here.

The message of conversion comes up against human [self] sufficiency in all its forms, from attachment to wealth to the proud assurance of the Pharisees. Jesus raises himself up like

the sign of Jonah in the midst of an evil generation [which
is] less well disposed towards God than Nineveh once was
(cf. Lk 11:29-32).[3]

Anyone who wishes to be a disciple of Christ has to understand
that it means seeing the world with a new sense of priorities and
a new kind of hope. It overturns things we take for granted. It
means the sort of leap of faith that the two disciples could not
make until 'they recognised him at the breaking of bread (cf. Lk
24:35). Up to that moment the amazing message that the women
had brought to the grieving community made no sense to them.
They had to meet the Risen Lord themselves.

The word which is used to describe the Christian task of
spreading the Good News is 'evangelisation'. But evangelisation
is not just the process of telling people that Jesus died and rose
again. That message had been passed on to the two disciples but
they were not yet evangelised. That happened only when they
recognised the Good News as the transformation of their lives and
as something that they had to share. Even though the day was
almost over even before they began their meal, as soon as they
really heard the Good News they set out that instant and returned
to Jerusalem to share their experience with the Apostles (cf. Lk
24:29, 33).

Overturned Expectations

Jesus repeatedly called his followers to an overturning of
expectations. There was the story about the admired, good-living
man praying familiarly with God and the despised tax collector
huddled at the back of the temple bemoaning his sins. Jesus drew
the lesson: 'This [sinful tax collector] went down to his house
justified rather than the other' (Lk 18:14; *New American Standard
Bible*). A poor woman diffidently put a few coppers on the plate

---

3. Xavier Léon-Dufour, 'Pénitence- Conversion', in *Vocabulaire de Théologie Biblique* (Paris:
Cerf, 1964), p. 794 (my translation).

among all the large gifts dropped in by wealthy people, but 'This poor widow has put in more than any of them' (Lk 21:3). It is not the woman who committed adultery but her accusers who slip away shame-facedly one by one (Jn 8:1-11). We will be judged not by how we treat the rich and the powerful and the admired, but by how we treat the least of his brothers and sisters (Mt 25:31-46).

Most importantly, what needs to be turned upside down is our own view of ourselves. St Paul put it memorably: 'God's foolishness is wiser than human wisdom and God's weakness is stronger than human strength [...] God chose what is foolish in the world to shame the wise; God chose what is weak in the world to shame the strong' (1 Cor 1:25, 28; NRSV). 'When I am weak, then I am strong' (2 Cor 12:10; NRSV).

The two disciples walking along the road could not grasp how what they had witnessed on Good Friday had overturned every preconception about what is possible. Jesus had been crucified. But they had not yet understood what they had seen. Far from being the end of their hopes, it was the weakness and foolishness of God shaming human wisdom and strength – the wisdom and strength of those who had condemned Jesus and the wisdom and strength of the two disciples. *All* human wisdom and *all* human strength had been shown to be unable to overcome God's love.

The Good News is not telling us that we are worthless and that our hopes are illusory. In fact, it tells us the very opposite. The Good News is that our hopes are not too big; they are too small. Nothing that we can imagine or achieve could ever be completely and permanently satisfying. But what the eye has not seen nor ear heard nor human heart conceived is already prepared by God for those who love him (cf. 1 Cor 2:9). All human strength is powerless to defeat death but God gives us the life over which death has no power (cf. Rom 6:9).

Human beings are a mixture of infinite longing on the one hand, and of all too finite achievements and disheartening failures on the other. That tension between longing and realisation is what gives life and energy to art and literature and every kind of creativity. We attempt to express who we are and how our hunger for perfect harmony, justice, beauty and truth stretches us; we try to articulate how agonisingly we are struck by the pain or inhumanity or injustice around us; we convey how we are moved by the love, the courage, the selflessness, the strength of conviction that show there is more to life than self-interest and short-term gain. We respond to a vision of who we are and who we can be.

In various artistic expressions we glimpse, at times with enormous poignancy and depth, some aspect of what is beyond our capacity fully to imagine or to express. But it remains only an aspect and it exists in the fragility of this world. Great pieces of music are lost; paintings are destroyed or stolen; beautiful buildings fall down. Shelley's vision of the broken statue lying in the ruins of a long-dead empire is true of every human construction:

> And on the pedestal these words appear:
> 'My name is Ozymandias, king of kings:
> Look on my works, ye Mighty, and despair!'
> Nothing beside remains. Round the decay
> of that colossal wreck, boundless and bare
> the lone and level sands stretch far away.[4]

The joyful experiences of life, the natural beauty of mountains and lakes, sunsets and snow-covered landscapes, the great human cultural achievements, the love that characterises our closest relationships with one another, can absorb our hearts and minds — but always with the hint of a longing for something more. If we fail to glimpse that longing, these absorbing realities can blind us to the greatness of the endless hope towards which they can only point.

---

4. Percy B. Shelley, extract from 'Ozymandias' (1819), in *The Penguin Book of English Verse*, ed. by J. Hayward (Harmondsworth: Penguin, 1936), p. 290.

Beginning in the Desert

The quest to understand what this means for the renewal of the Church and for the renewal of each individual member starts in the deserts of which Benedict XVI spoke as he began his ministry as Pope. It is no accident that he began that reflection with dramatic words about how Jesus seeks the sheep which is wandering in the desert: 'He leaps to his feet and abandons the glory of heaven, in order to go in search of the [lost] sheep and pursue it, all the way to the Cross.'[5] Our quest for God is first of all God's quest for us; what we find is the God who first loved us.

It was in the desert, where the Spirit led him to be tempted, that Jesus began his ministry. The account of the temptation is not just an event at the beginning of his public life: it poses and answers the fundamental questions about the mission of Jesus and about human life:

> Matthew and Luke recount three temptations of Jesus that reflect the inner struggle over his own particular mission and, at the same time, address the question as to what truly matters in human life. At the heart of all temptations, as we see here, is the act of pushing God aside because we perceive him as secondary, if not actually superfluous and annoying, in comparison with all the apparently far more urgent matters that fill our lives. Constructing a world by our own lights, without reference to God, building our own foundation; refusing to acknowledge the reality of anything beyond the political and material, while setting God aside as an illusion – that is the temptation that threatens us in many varied forms.[6]

In rejecting the temptations to possessions (turning stones into bread), prestige (leaping down spectacularly from the temple

---

5. Homily at Mass for the Inauguration of his Pontificate, 24 April 2005.
6. J. Ratzinger, Benedict XVI, *Jesus of Nazareth*, trans. by J. A. Walker (London: Bloomsbury, 2007), p. 28.

borne up by angels) and power (ruling all the kingdoms of the world), Jesus did not suggest that any of these were bad in themselves. He insisted that he would never put them in the place of God. We must try to live not on bread alone but on God's word; we must not seek to use God to make us look good in the eyes of others; God alone is the source of human power and we must serve him alone (cf. Mt 4:1-11).

These are the temptations that threaten all of his followers and with particular force they can seduce those of us who live in secularised societies which accord God, at best, only a limited, private space. These are temptations by which the message and mission of the Good News can be distorted. They are the temptations that challenge individuals, communities and the Church as a whole.

The temptations in the desert are at the heart of the challenge of following him faithfully. A secularised culture may profess to be very tolerant towards religious belief, unless it 'intrudes' in some way. For the believer, however, the Creator can never be an intruder in creation, can never be confined to a private space. God is either the One who creates and sustains the whole of creation and every aspect of it, or not God at all.

St Paul wrote to the Thessalonians: 'As soon as you heard the message that we brought you as God's message, you accepted it for what it really is, God's message and not some human thinking; and it is still a living power among you who believe it' (1 Thess 2:13; *Jerusalem Bible*). The Good News is not one item among many, which can be allowed to take a subordinate position in society and in the lives of individuals provided it 'behaves itself'. It is not some human plan or thinking. It is the Word through whom all things were made and through whom creation is renewed, the Word who became flesh and lived and died among us, the Word who is now in the glory that he had with his Father before the world was made (cf. Jn 17:5).

Serving God Alone

The fundamental temptation is to allow something to take the place of God, to allow anything to obscure the place of God in our lives. The difficulty is that so many things already do come between us and God, often in ways that we fail to recognise.

I was once present in a group discussing care of the dying. At the beginning of a talk by a palliative care consultant, everyone was asked to list five points under a number of headings: people I love, places that mean most to me, activities I enjoy, possessions that I value, abilities and skills that are important to me. As his talk proceeded, the consultant would tell us, at random intervals, to cross out one of these items. The process became very painful, almost impossible, as one reached the most important entries under each heading, and especially under the heading 'people I love'. Each of us has a number of people, a variety of supports and capacities on which we rely. Even as part of what was merely an exercise, striking a line through some of those names felt like an act of deep betrayal. However generous our love of God, there will always be things we are unwilling to give up. We hold back on acknowledging that God is more important than any created reality because we are afraid that the Lord might test our sincerity. But God is our only hope and the only hope of those we love.

Repentance, seeing things differently, means recognising our blind spots; it means upending our assumptions. The trouble is that it is impossible for us to fully stand outside our culture and therefore to stand outside our assumptions. Our culture can influence our perceptions, because we take it for granted – as the fish does with the water – until, perhaps too late, we recognise the ways in which it is poisoning us.

> We assume that language is neutral – what else could it be? We choose words, don't we, to say what we please? But language really works as a kind of tramline that takes us each time along a pre-ordained course. Language, supplied to us from some central repository, comes replete with definitions

of reality, and perspectives on reality, which do not make themselves visible in the words they infect, but nevertheless condition the result: the thought conceived in the words.[7]

One has to ask questions about some of the assumptions on which our society operates: is it the case that we value people by their wealth, by their celebrity and by their influence?[8] Is it the case that we imagine that social life can operate very comfortably when the question of God and faith is seen as irrelevant? In our individual lives is it true that we sometimes behave at work, in sport and in political life without any reference to our belief and trust in God who gives meaning to every moment of life? What does it really mean to observe the fundamental commandment that we are to love God with all our heart and all our soul and all our mind and all our strength (cf. Mk 12:30)?

Is that belief, trust and commitment recognised as the meaning of everything that takes place in every aspect of what we consciously do as Church members – in the structural dimension, in what we see as parish life, even in our celebration of liturgy? Every renewal should be at the service of a growth in union with Christ, otherwise it is an empty shell:

> Let us have no illusions: unless we follow this spiritual path, external structures of communion will serve very little purpose. They would become mechanisms without a soul, 'masks' of communion rather than its means of expression and growth.[9]

It may seem that these considerations are some distance away from the urgent questions of renewal of the structures and the organisation of the Church. Many of those who are deeply

---

7. John P. Waters, *Beyond Consolation* (London: Continuum, 2010), p. 63.
8. On this, see Alain de Botton, *Status Anxiety* (London: Hamilton, 2004), passim.
9. *Novo millennio ineunte*, 43.

concerned about the future of the Church say that if a business were losing market share at the same rate as the Church, it would be doing everything from revamping its logo to slashing its workforce to updating its product in order to make it attractive for a new situation. But first we have to ask ourselves what the Church is meant to be and to do. Only in the light of serious reflection and prayer about that can we hope to bring about reforms that will bear fruit. Being successful in terms of the possessions, prestige and power with which Jesus was tempted in the desert cannot be the answer to the question of what the Church is meant to be.

On his flight to the United Kingdom for his visit in September 2010, Pope Benedict was asked how the Church might become more credible and attractive. His reply went to the heart of the matter:

> I would say that a church which seeks above all to be attractive would already be on the wrong path, because the Church does not work for itself, does not work to increase its numbers so as to have more power. The Church is at the service of Another; it does not serve itself, seeking to be a strong body, but it strives to make the Gospel of Jesus Christ accessible [...] In this sense, the Church does not seek to be attractive, but rather to make herself transparent for Jesus Christ.[10]

The first step has to be to listen again to the radical invitation to leave all things and follow him (cf. Mk 20:28). That is the invitation on which the Church is built. Every member is called to a following that recognises Jesus, the Son of God, as the Lord of creation. We are called to see him also as the one who poured out his Blood in agony to show us that God's love is large enough to embrace, heal and perfect every human being and the whole human family. No person, no thing, no plan, no relationship, no

---

10. Meeting with journalists, 16 September 2010.

power can come between us and the love of God made visible in Christ Jesus (cf. Rom 8:39).

All that we accomplish, all that we value, all that is good in human life we will find once again, free from sin and weakness and corruption, 'illuminated and transfigured'.[11] In order to be part of the new creation all the fruits of our efforts need to be transfigured – every trace of selfishness and every danger of destruction, every way in which they may harm others have to be removed. In other words, they must die and rise again to the life where death, mourning and weeping are no more (cf. Rev 21:3, 4). That is why, in the words that opened this chapter, the poet prays for the death and rebirth of all that is important to us and in us:

> O years that certainly will bless
>> Our flowers with fruits, our seeds with flowers,
> *With ruin all our perfectness.*

We are unable to construct this new creation; it is not an accomplishment on our part, but a gift from God. So we want what we accomplish to be blessed with ruin and with new life. When the Pharisee proudly presented to God all the good things he had done, his fundamental failure was that he had no appreciation of how empty they were unless they were efforts to respond to the transforming gift of God and of how God could 'illuminate and transfigure' those efforts.

If we did not begin here, we would miss the point entirely. We would fail to see that the foundation of everything is the love of God for us.[12] We would fail to be open to the mystery of God and to the presence of God in each of us. Without that, all the efforts we make at building up our faith community would go for nothing; the resultant structures 'would become mechanisms without a soul'.[13]

---

11. *Gaudium et spes*, 39.
12. See *Deus caritas est*, 1.
13. *Novo millennio ineunte*, 43.

A Prayer in Weakness

God our Father,

you have invited us to share your life.

No words of ours could ever express the greatness of the
destiny you offer us;

no effort of ours could bring about the new life that is your
gift.

Help us to understand this not as a humiliation but as our
glory.

Help us to trust in you rather than in our ability

and to know that our talents are not our own achievements
but your gifts.

Even your weakness and your foolishness

are stronger than our strength and our wisdom.[14]

We hope in a new creation that is beyond our power to
construct.

All that we could hope for — and infinitely more — awaits us.

May we see that hope for what it is: your loving and
undeserved gift.

When we are weak or shattered, when our hopes seem vain,

you invite us to see things in a different light —

in the light of your Son who endured for our sake

agony, betrayal, injustice, mockery and cruel death.

Help us to trust in the light that shines in his life, death and
resurrection,

the light which darkness cannot overpower.

Amen.

---

14. Cf. 1 Cor 1:25.

CHAPTER THREE

God's Most Stupendous Attribute

Maybe it is here he must search
In this hell of unfaith
Where no one has a purpose
Where the web of Meaning is broken threads
And one man looks at another in fear.
O God can a man find You when he lies with his face
  downwards
And his nose in the rubble that was his achievement?
Is the music playing behind the door of despair?
O God give us purpose.[1]

Not Humiliation but Reconciliation

We cannot rely on our own 'perfectness'. That realisation prompts us to recognise that we must look to a greater source of hope. The twelve steps of Alcoholics Anonymous[2] are based on the recognition by the alcoholic of the bleak emptiness and the powerless fantasy that underlie his or her illusion of perfectness. The twelve steps, however, are not just for alcoholics. They spell out the elements of repentance. We admit our powerlessness; we

---

1. Patrick Kavanagh, extract from 'From Failure Up'.
2. See http://www.aa.org/en__pdfs/smf-121__en.pdf.

believe and trust in a Power greater than ourselves; we ask God to forgive our sins and remove our defects; we seek through prayer and meditation to draw closer to God and to know and live his will.

Repentance is a humbling experience, but not a humiliating one. Humiliation suggests that other people have grounds to look down on the one who is humbled. But no human being is in a position to look down on anybody else unless they meet the criterion demanded by Jesus for those who would cast the first stone (cf. Jn 8:7). Of course anyone who believes that he has met that criterion is deceiving himself (cf. 1 Jn 1:8).

Conversion or repentance is also reconciliation. It involves our opening of ourselves to God's ever-present love. At the same time, it involves opening ourselves to those who have offended us and to those we have offended. The person who is reconciled may be more humbled than ever if he or she is generously forgiven, but forgiveness does not humiliate; rather it restores one's self-respect.

It may be that the offended person is not willing, or not yet ready to forgive. Then one can only wait in hope for that gift. God's love, however, is always offered.

The desire to humiliate another human being is itself a fault; the search for justice should not be confused with the seeking of revenge. At its best the quest for justice is an invitation to restore friendship and love. The ultimate peace and healing we seek are the utterly undeserved gift of God. We are not in competition with one another for that gift, nor are we judges of one another's worthiness. We can only receive God's mercy when we are prepared to rejoice in our reception of the gift together with all humanity, including people of whom we disapprove, whom we dislike, against whom we have a grievance.

Looking at another human being with contempt is a failure to understand that he or she has been offered God's gift along with ourselves, and that our invitation includes a requirement that we share that gift with all those to whom God offers it. We have no more claim on that free gift than they have. We need God's mercy and it is both idle and harmful to speculate about whether others need it more or less than we. The reality is that we would all be lost without it.

The Quality of Mercy

The gift which calls us and enables us to repent, the gift which opens us up to the fulfilment of all our longing, is mercy. Pope John Paul described mercy as: 'the most stupendous attribute of the Creator and the Redeemer.'[3] Mercy is received by a person who is repentant – and that repentance is itself God's gift. Forgiveness is always a gift. It is never possible to approach another human being, still less the infinite God, saying, 'I demand that you forgive me'. Some of the greatest thinkers of antiquity believed in a god or gods, but not that the gods could have an interest in and commitment to the welfare of individual creatures, not to speak of having unlimited love for them. They would have understood how stupendous, how hard to grasp, is the claim that God is merciful and forgiving towards those who offend, insult or reject him.

Because we are finite, suffering and pain are part of every life: suffering inflicted on us; suffering we inflict on others; suffering that follows from being mortal and vulnerable. We cannot remove all evil from the world because we are limited in our ability to control events, the outcomes of our actions or those of others or the forces of nature; we cannot eliminate the power of evil and the pain of suffering: 'Only God is able to do this: only a God who personally enters history by making himself man and suffering within history.'[4]

The Pharisee praying in the temple made two related mistakes. He inflated his own view of himself, imagining that God would be impressed by the list of his religious observances. At the same time he scorned the tax collector, presuming that God must despise

---

3. John Paul II, *Dives in misericordia*, 13.
4. Benedict XVI, *Spe salvi*, 36.

such a poor specimen of humanity. Those thoughts corrupted his prayer. Similar attitudes, maybe cleverly disguised even from ourselves, are certainly present in ours.

The power of the parable lies in the fact that the first listeners would instinctively have shared the Pharisee's reading of the situation. If, however, we pray like the tax collector, 'God, be merciful to me, a sinner' (Lk 18:13), then comparing oneself favourably to other seekers of mercy cannot form any part of our attitude. We must not silently make an addition to our prayer, 'God be merciful to me — but we both know there are certain people we could name who are a lot worse than me!'

We do not know how other people stand with God. We are tempted, for instance, to presume that those who do not believe in God are much further from him than we are. The truth may be that what they reject is a mistaken image of God — for instance a god who is unforgiving or uncaring, so that what they deny is not 'the God of the Gospels'. Sometimes that mistaken image may be projected by believers, who by our unconvincing lives may 'conceal rather than reveal the true nature of God'.[5] In a particularly harmful way we project such an image when we refuse to forgive or when we mark people out as 'hopeless cases'. Then we have embraced an image of God as unforgiving, and of ourselves as being in no need of forgiveness.

As We Forgive

We have begun to understand God's mercy only when we are able to ask the Father to 'forgive us *as we forgive those who trespass against us*'. This too is a crucial element in the renewal of the Church in every generation and in every situation. It was expressed in a challenging manner by Cardinal Giovanni Battista Montini, later Pope Paul VI, in an address to the preachers of a mission in Milan:

---

5. See *Gaudium et spes*, 19.

I believe that so many errors, misunderstandings and attacks can, in these times, be dealt with more efficaciously with goodness than polemics [...] Let no one be offended, feel irony, feel himself attacked by our preaching; let them feel on the contrary that they are invited and expected.[6]

St Francis de Sales is quoted as saying: 'Always be as gentle as you can and remember that one catches more flies with a spoonful of honey than with a hundred barrels of vinegar.' This is not just advice for preachers; it is what is required of the entire Christian community. If those who feel themselves distant from the Church perceive the attitude of individuals, groups, organisations or Catholic publications as harsh, if they detect an attitude of hostility and distrust, of glee at any perceived embarrassment of the 'enemy', or a feeling that 'when you left the Church it was no loss', they will hardly feel 'invited and expected'.

If we wish to be forgiven *as we forgive*, then we must take very seriously what Cardinal Montini said to priests who felt under attack from the hostility they encountered. The Christian, and particularly the priest, has to see the world with the eyes of mercy and compassion:

> We will have a passionate love of souls, of the society that surrounds us. We will love all those whom we approach and who may have contempt for us, hinder us, perhaps even offend us. But we will never be able to feel offended. The less we are loved, the more we will love. The more difficult it becomes to remain in contact with the world, the more we will love. The more difficult it becomes to free the world of its illusions of happiness, self-sufficiency, satisfaction, the more we will love it. We will seek to overcome all with love. 'Charity overcomes all things.'[7]

---

6. Giovanni Cardinal Montini, *The Priest* (Dublin: Helicon, 1965), p. 168.
7. Ibid., pp. 62–3.

Labouring for the Conversion of Sinners

It is a difficult ideal. But it is a most important one. There are many things to be said about the decline in the celebration of the sacrament of reconciliation, and many reasons that might be suggested for it. Among the reasons is a failure to find a way of expressing in our lives what is stated by the Second Vatican Council:

> Those who approach the sacrament of Penance obtain pardon from God's mercy for the offence committed against him, and are, at the same time, reconciled to the Church which they have wounded by their sins and which by charity, by example and by prayer labours for their conversion.[8]

The community of faith, the individuals, the families, the parishes, the dioceses, the universal Church are meant to be labouring for the conversion of sinners by love, example and prayer. We are all meant to be signs of the unfailing generosity of God's mercy. If we were really doing that, then those who had offended or failed people, or betrayed the Gospel message, or set out to cause ill-feeling and trouble (all of us in different ways at different times) would feel 'invited and expected' to return. We would feel the warmth of an invitation to rejoice in the mercy of God, to renew our commitment to the mission of the Church. Ultimately, it is not a question of 'us and them'. In this life all of us are dependent on the mercy of God. The parable of the Pharisee and the tax collector rebukes all who think that they are better than others, however disreputable or hostile the others may seem. Jesus was challenged about his readiness to eat with tax collectors and public sinners; he replied that he had come to those who were sinners (cf. Mk 2:15-17, Mt 9:10-13).

Our society is full of people who are broken or distressed or lost; sometimes they suffer invisibly. We are meant to be a people

---

8. *Lumen gentium*, 11.

and a community who make it possible for men and women to glimpse through us and through the life of our faith community the unlimited and unshakeable mercy of God for them. Could it be that a person might come to Mass, laden with guilt, and feel that he or she was out of place among these 'holy' people who did not seem to have time or understanding for someone deeply troubled by guilt? Such a person should rather feel welcome and should be able to sense already in the Penitential Rite, and throughout the celebration, that he or she is among people who know that their only ultimate hope lies not in their 'perfectness' but in the forgiveness that their God offers to all who turn to him.

Might it be that some of the fall away from the sacrament of penance is due not just to the inertia or lack of understanding of those who have stopped coming, but to the failure of those who have not shown them the face of the merciful God visible in the life of the Church? How else can one explain the fact that the sacrament continues to flourish in places of pilgrimage, where the pilgrim is surrounded by the prayer of pilgrims who have come to express their trust in God's merciful love, and their prayer for God's mercy not only for themselves but for their fellow pilgrims?

This points to another reason for the decline in the reception of the sacrament. The sacrament of reconciliation is, like all sacraments, a liturgical act. The Second Vatican Council said that 'the sacred liturgy is above all things the worship of the divine Majesty'.[9] The worship of God is the focus of the whole pilgrimage, as it is of the sacrament of penance. This is a truth that needs to be better understood. The centre of attention of the sacrament is not the sinner, still less the sins. The focus, as in all acts of worship, is on God. The penitent sinner is, first and foremost, praising the mercy of God – praising God in particular because of the mercy which is freeing him or her from the sins that are being brought to the healing power of that stupendous attribute.

9. Second Vatican Council, *Sacrosanctum concilium*, 33.

The challenge on each Christian to be a sign of mercy may seem vague. What does it require of us? What can any individual do about it? Why not wait until the parish priest, the parish pastoral council, the bishop tell us what we need to do? But this is not, in the first instance, about what we do; it is about who we are and about how our faith can be or can fail to be visible in our lives.

We are meant to be a community that shows the merciful face of the Good Shepherd. The hardest step in that is to be ready to forgive those who have deeply hurt us. Even within Church organisations, it may be hard to show a welcome to a person who has blocked what we regard as our far-seeing proposals and our best efforts. It is difficult when we feel personally hurt by what we see as a deliberate wounding insult. We can weave beautiful words about the quality of mercy in the abstract, but there will be moments when the demands will seem unreasonable: 'Forgive! After what he did to me, after what she said about me, after all I have suffered? You must be joking!' I may be convinced that I am entirely in the right and that it is entirely up to the other person to take the first step: 'I have nothing to apologise for.' It is, of course, not entirely inconceivable that the other person may be proclaiming, and believing, a similar tale of injured innocence.

Hurt and Healing

There is a particular problem when people feel they have been injured by the Church community or by individual members of it, or by Church discipline, with regard to admission to the reception of the Eucharist, or Church teachings on sexuality or the indissolubility of marriage. There are those who have felt insulted when they approached a representative of the Church. Misunderstandings occur in the Church as in every human community, but the atmosphere should be one in which misunderstanding or even intended hurts should be overwhelmed by the practical longing for reconciliation and renewal. The healing love of God reaches out to everyone – not just to those who suffer because of their own wrongdoing but to those whose suffering is inflicted by others and even to those who deliberately cause pain to others.

People who suffered sexual abuse as children at the hands of clergy or religious or in a Church-run institution face a real contradiction. The Church, which is the sign of God's unlimited love and healing, is for them the context for betrayal of their trust and the destruction of their lives. The sign of God's healing love is obscured by the horrors perpetrated by those who represented it. This is multiplied by failures and errors of Church authorities in dealing with abusers or in recognising the hurt of survivors.

There are very many people in society who were abused as children in other contexts. They too should find in the Christian community an appreciation of their suffering, an affirmation of their worth; they should see in the community a sign of healing and a willingness to lead towards the full reconciliation with people who, for a whole variety of reasons, did not support them as they would have expected, and reconciliation perhaps even with their abusers.

Anyone who has been so cruelly mistreated as a child has every right to feel a deep anger and a sense of utter betrayal. Their trust has been heartlessly violated. The road to peace may be long, possibly lifelong. But it will, please God, lead towards a situation where, without forgetting or overlooking the wrong, the survivor recognises his or her inner dignity and strength; there may come a serenity where a person's life is not consumed by events which were in no way their doing. In some cases, with the help of God and of good friends and a supportive community, it may even lead to the ability to forgive their abuser. This is a process that cannot be short-circuited. Reconciliation is a kind of sharing in the Resurrection, in new life. We fully reach that new life only when we have followed Christ through death. All of us, and in a particular way the survivors of childhood abuse, live in the in-between of Holy Saturday.

People have felt hurt or insulted by a priest; people feel unwanted and excluded by the community which is supposed to be labouring towards their reconciliation. In every community there are injuries and scars. In every group unity is broken, harmony is disturbed and pain is inflicted. How can any community be a sign of healing mercy without limit?

The mercy that can fully free us does not come from ourselves. That is true whether we are trapped in our own wrongdoing or whether we are trapped in the wrongdoing that others have done to us. The mercy of God is more powerful than any evil. Its goal is greater than we can envisage. The goal is the forgiveness of our sinfulness, the healing of our suffering; but it is more: God's mercy seeks the healing of those we have hurt and of those who have hurt us. God seeks the reconciliation which will be celebrated in the new creation when people of every race, time and culture will be one. God 'desires everyone to be saved and to come to the knowledge of the truth' (1 Tim 2:4; NRSV).

We all experience an unwillingness to forgive those who hurt us. It is not easy to forgive a wrong that has caused incalculable pain to ourselves and to those we love. We say, 'I could never forgive'. We may find it virtually impossible to approach those we have offended. Our difficulties are understandable, but they are also a sign that we have not grasped the greatness of God's offer. God reaches out to everyone; my inability to do so shows me that I have not yet fully understood the wonder of God's most stupendous attribute. In heaven we will see the presence of such people not as an insult to us but as a sign of the limitless quality of God's love. The truth is that no living person is beyond redemption. Whenever I think that I would not be willing to share eternal life with somebody, I am being invited to believe that God is even more merciful than I have yet grasped. That is the source of hope for all of us.

Moses raised a bronze serpent in the desert as a sign and guarantee of God's power to heal even deadly bites from 'fiery serpents':

> We see clearly that man cannot save himself from the consequences of his sin. He cannot save himself from death.

Only God can release him from his moral and physical enslavement. And because he loved the world so much, he sent his only-begotten Son, not to condemn the world – as justice seemed to demand – but so that through him the world might be saved. God's only-begotten Son had to be lifted up just as Moses lifted up the serpent in the desert, so that all who looked upon him with faith might have life.[10]

One thing that needs strengthening in the Church of the twenty-first century in Ireland and, I suspect, much further afield, is a clear grasp of what Pope Benedict is saying here. This is the fundamental overturning of human expectations and hopes that calls us to conversion. This is the revelation of the only hope that can fully satisfy us. Humanity has achieved many wonders, not least in overcoming some of the greatest threats to human happiness and in opening up new possibilities – in the treatment of diseases, in communications, in scientific discoveries. But our fundamental weakness remains: we cannot give meaning to our own lives, we must find the meaning which the Creator has revealed in creation and in the many ways God spoke to our ancestors and finally in his Son (cf. Heb 1:1-2).

That is the newness that we have to allow to change us, to penetrate us. Then we will begin to see the scale and the depth of the renewal that we need in our individual lives and in our Church. It will be a renewal constantly stirred and enthused by the wonder of our belief in the transforming power of 'the wondrous Cross'.

The Cross, then, is something far greater and more mysterious than it at first appears. It is indeed an instrument of torture, suffering and defeat, but at the same time it expresses the complete transformation, the definitive reversal of these evils: that is what makes it the most eloquent symbol of hope that the world has ever seen. It speaks to all who

---

10. Benedict XVI, Homily at the Church of the Holy Cross, Nicosia, Cyprus, 5 June 2010.

suffer — the oppressed, the sick, the poor, the outcast, the victims of violence — and it offers them hope that God can transform their suffering into joy, their isolation into communion, their death into life. It offers unlimited hope to our fallen world.[11]

Here a practical question arises. What kind of renewal can allow our communities to show more clearly this 'most eloquent symbol of hope', especially for those who feel excluded and who do not see that mercy as transforming their lives? Do we need new structures or new attitudes? Clearly we need both.

The question requires honest, painful reflection as individuals, as groups and as a parish community about how we look to people on the edges of the Church, 'hanging on by their fingernails'. What about the people who are hostile and alienated? What about the people whose lives are in a mess, socially, financially? Who are those people in our parish or area? Do they see the welcoming, open arms of people who by love, example and prayer have laboured to invite them to share our faith and our hope? If that is not the case, the loss consists not only in the fact that such people will not feel invited, but in the reality that our parish or area is failing in its call to be the sign and the celebration of Christ's presence. The mercy of God is seen not only in the forgiveness of sins but in the gifts that he gives to individuals and communities. To be a sign of that mercy means appreciating and nourishing those gifts. Through the Cross, the merciful love of God 'expresses the complete transformation, the definitive reversal of evil'.

Every parish needs to have a pastoral council or a body which looks seriously at how the life of the parish can be expressive of that transformation. One of its priorities should be to look at those who may not feel welcome or wanted and to see how they can be encouraged and made to feel at home. There will be other more specific means to express that welcome and belonging — groups

---

11. Ibid.

for liturgy, bereavement, prayer, *Lectio divina*, baptism preparation, youth, welcoming new arrivals or groups to reach out to families and individuals who are economically and socially marginalised. There is no end to the ways in which parish communities can seek to ensure that they are perceived as signs of the welcoming, merciful, stupendous love of God. The task for every Christian community is to let God's love and mercy speak to its own members and to the world.

It is unmistakably clear that the future vitality of the Church in Ireland will depend on the existence of structures such as the parish pastoral council. These will have to look realistically at how the parish can be what it is meant to be — a community aware of the greatness of God's mercy. It is one of the fundamental roles of priests and of parish communities to foster, draw out and develop the variety and range of gifts that the Holy Spirit has given to every community so that it can live and share the Good News:

> Priests must sincerely acknowledge and promote the dignity of the laity and the part proper to them in the mission of the Church. And they should hold in high honour that just freedom which is due to everyone in the earthly city [...] While trying the spirits to see if they be of God, priests should uncover with a sense of faith, acknowledge with joy and foster with diligence the various humble and exalted charisms of the laity.[12]

Undoubtedly there are situations where people feel that they are not receiving much encouragement to engage in such initiatives. The first response is to recognise that each Christian is commissioned in baptism to go out and spread the Good News of the transformation expressed by the Cross. That does not require anybody's permission or encouragement.

---

12. Second Vatican Council, *Presbyterorum ordinis*, 9.

One of the benefits of the restructuring that is taking place in many dioceses through the establishment of pastoral areas will be that such initiatives will in future tend to be based not just on individual parishes with what sometimes seem to be impermeable borders but in wider areas where the variety of gifts may have wider scope.

Prayer in Praise of God's Mercy
Almighty God,
we see the wonder of your power
in the mountains, in the mighty seas,
in the rich variety of life on earth,
in the unimaginable vastness of the universe.
We thank you for your creation with all its marvels.
The most stupendous sign of your power
is the unfailing mercy you offer us when we sin against you.
It is because you are all-powerful that you are merciful to all:
'Disposing of such strength, you are mild in judgement,
You govern us with great lenience.'[13]
God of mercy and compassion,
awaken in us an ever-deeper gratitude for the gift
of your merciful love.
May we forgive those who offend us
with a generosity inspired by your infinite mercy
on which all our hope is founded.
Amen.

---

13. Wisdom 12:16-19.

CHAPTER FOUR

The Sleeping Giant

The laity in the Church are like a sleeping giant, over seven hundred million strong. They can do immense work for the Kingdom of God, but they must first be fully awakened [...] When one recalls the high hopes of twenty years ago,[1] it is sad to have to admit that the laity in most parishes are still a largely untapped resource.[2]

Waking Up to the Good News

The late Cardinal Ó Fiaich's striking image of the sleeping giant is a description not only of the laity but of the whole Church – laity, religious and clergy. We are not fully awake to the reality that surrounds us and is within us. We are still walking the road to Emmaus. Our hearts may burn from time to time; there are occasions when we recognise the beauty of God's creation, when we give heartfelt thanks for families and friends and so on, when we pray intensely for someone who is seriously ill, but a great deal of the time we are scarcely conscious of the transforming presence of the One who has overturned everything and who walks with us at every moment. The two disciples heard the Good News as a confusing, puzzling statement. That is not enough. We need to be overturned; we need to change.

---

1. The reference is to the Second Vatican Council, which closed in 1965.
2. Cardinal Tomás Ó Fiaich, *Intervention at Synod of Bishops* (1987).

Hearing the Good News is not just an intellectual exercise or the result of theological study. It bears fruit in the reflection and openness which spiritual writers have called contemplation. In that reflection we recognise our weakness before the great questions of life, and in that weakness we recognise the strength which is God's gift of love:

> [The contemplative outlook] is the outlook of those who do not presume to take possession of reality but instead accept it as a gift, discovering in all things the reflection of the Creator and seeing in every person his living image.[3]

Really to hear the Good News means being profoundly altered by it. It means seeing everything in a new light. But even as we seek to repent, to change our heart and mind, we remain always to some extent dozing. We are always travellers along the road to repentance. Only in the eternal light of the new creation will we fully awaken.

But we could be a good deal more awake than we are! To be awake means knowing that the love of God is the most important reality in our lives. It means knowing that truth is not just an important fact to be filed away; it means knowing it with our heart and soul and mind and strength.

Our knowledge of God is expressed not just in doctrines, but in worship, in living, in relationships, in art and poetry, in recreation, in working for justice and peace, in celebrating the image of God in human beings, in how we live. It is not just the most important of many calls on our energy commitment and belief, not just another item on the agenda. None of the other calls or items on the agenda fully make sense except in the context of the invitation to receive and share God's love. The believer knows that even the love of parents, spouse, siblings and closest friends depends entirely on God the Creator. Our love for them wants the

---

3. John Paul II, *Evangelium vitae*, 83.

best for them; we want them to find the fulfilment of their deepest hope. But we cannot give that fulfilment to them or ensure it for them. They can receive it only from the gift of God's love. We want to participate in that fulfilment with them. Only God's unlimited mercy can and does offer a life of eternal joy to them and to us.

These are not just words. Unless there is a renewal of a faith that accepts God's word for what it really is, namely the creative and redemptive meaning of human life and of every corner of every human life, there will be no renewal in the Church.

> The Church must speak of many things: of all the issues connected with the human being, of her own structure and of the way she is ordered and so forth. But her true and – under various aspects – only theme is 'God'. Moreover, the great problem of the West is forgetfulness of God. This forgetfulness is spreading. In short, all the individual problems can be traced back to this question, I am sure of it.[4]

The Gospel is not communicated as 'what it really is' unless it is recognised as being about the whole of human life and the whole of its meaning. The person who is convinced of that truth is one who knows that our real strength is not our own and that when we are weak, then we are strong; then we can discover where our real strength lies.

One of the most important items on the agenda of the renewal of the Church in Ireland is to reflect on the Good News and to try to learn what the mission we have received in baptism calls us to do. In the light of that reflection and learning we try to work out together what initiatives and what renewal of priorities and structures in the parish or in the diocese or in the country are needed to do that more effectively. Pope John Paul said in Knock that this is a permanent mission of the Church which 'must constantly look for new ways that will enable her to understand

---

4. Benedict XVI, Address to the Members of the Roman Curia, 22 December 2006.

more profoundly and to carry out with renewed vigour the mission received from her Founder'.[5] This renewal has to awaken the giant in each of us and in each of our families and communities. However weak we are, we are a giant animated by the strength, or better the Spirit, of God. The awakened giant is the Body of Christ living and active in the world.

The image of the awakened giant may, however, be seriously misunderstood. It does not imply that the Church can or should expect to be always, or even usually, triumphant. The Church is founded on the love revealed when Jesus, placing God his Father before all else, hung on the Cross. There he renounced the human possessions and prestige and power which would never be allowed stand between him and his Father. On the Cross he showed most clearly what he had declared in the desert at the beginning of his ministry. Nothing must come between us and the love of God.

It is not about victory in terms of human calculation. If we allow our appreciation of the gift of God to become a source of smugness or complacency, we have entirely misunderstood it. This is not about how wonderful we are; it is about how wonderful God is. Otherwise we fall back into the illusion of self-sufficiency that blinds us to our need of God's gift.

We also forget how the giant can be weakened by sleepiness, sinfulness and lack of repentance in his constituent parts. 'We have this treasure in earthen vessels, to show that the transcendent power belongs to God and not to us' (2 Cor 4:7).

Listening to the Word

In failure and weakness, in the ruin of our perfectness, we can become more ready to appreciate our need of the transcendent power of endlessly merciful love. The Church has to remember the lesson of the temptation in the desert. She does not exist in order to be popular or powerful or comfortable.[6]

---

5. Homily at Knock, 30 September 1979.
6. In an interview given by Pope Benedict XVI on a plane journey to the United Kingdom, 16 September 2010.

The first step in any renewal is to listen in order to hear — not just with our minds but with our hearts and souls and strength — what Pope Benedict called 'the heart of the Christian faith' which shows us 'the Christian image of God and the resulting image of mankind and its destiny'. He goes on:

> *We have come to believe in God's love:* in these words the Christian can express the fundamental decision of his life. Being a Christian is not the result of an ethical choice or a lofty idea, but the encounter with an event, a person, which gives life a new horizon and a decisive direction.[7]

The foundation of the Christian life is a meeting with a person, Jesus Christ, and with the events of his life, death and resurrection by which he transformed everything and gives life a new horizon and direction. That is the Good News that the two disciples finally understood when they recognised him 'in the breaking of bread' (Lk 24:35). The renewal of the Church in any place or time has to be based on that same recognition.

It is worth noticing the reasons given by Pope Benedict for writing his first encyclical on the theme 'God is Love':

> In a world where the name of God is sometimes associated with vengeance or even a duty of hatred and violence, this message is both timely and significant. For this reason, I wish in my first Encyclical to speak of the love which God lavishes upon us and which we in turn must share with others.[8]

Anyone who has heard the Good News about God's love knows that it is meant to be shared with other people. The sleeping giant would really awaken if every member of the Church were responding to that duty, which is not so much a duty as the

---

7. *Deus caritas est*, 1 (italics in original).
8. Ibid.

overflowing of the love lavished on us. Where will those who do not know Christ in our society, or who know him only like the two disciples, dimly and without conviction, be able to meet the challenge and hope of the Good News? If the love lavished on us is carefully guarded in case it might cause offence, or shielded like some secret information to be kept to ourselves, how will they encounter Jesus who is the answer to every human hope?

Letting Love Speak
That does not mean that we should be always speaking explicitly about God. Obviously, not every situation provides a suitable context for a sermon. There are obviously limits of courtesy and appropriateness as to when and how we should speak:

> A Christian knows when it is time to speak of God and when it is better to let love alone speak. He knows that God is love and that God's presence is felt at the very time when the only thing to do is love.[9]

There are many ways to let love speak. Sometimes we fail to recognise the value and extent of what seem to be very ordinary, insignificant forms of witness to the Gospel. John the Baptist was troubled because the world seemed not to have changed after the coming of Christ. He sent two of this followers to ask, 'Are you the one who is to come, or shall we look for another?' (Lk 7:19). Down the centuries the promise of changing the world has been made by ideologues and dictators who brought instead destruction and emptiness. Pope Benedict poses the Baptist's question for today:

> We should again see Christ and ask: 'Are you the one?' The Lord, in his own silent way responds, 'You see what I have

---

9. Ibid., 31c.

done. I have not brought a revolution of bloodshed. I have not changed the world by force, but I have lit so many lights which in the intervening time form a great road of light down the millennia [...] It is not the great promises that change the world but the silent light of the truth, of the goodness of God which is the sign of his presence and gives us the assurance that we are loved to the end [...][10]

The first place we should witness is in our daily lives. We are called to live as followers of Christ in *every corner and aspect* of our lives. The life of the parish is not just what goes on in the church or in events organised by the priest or the parish pastoral council. Whenever a Christian behaves as a good neighbour, he or she is fulfilling the vocation that comes through the sacraments of baptism and confirmation, and is living as a member of the Eucharistic community. Whenever a Christian tries to behave conscientiously and justly at work or in any involvement with others, witness is given to the Gospel and the life of the parish and the whole Church is enriched. Anyone who reaches out to someone who is poor, troubled or grief-stricken is taking an active part in the life of the parish. But that participation will be all the richer if one recognises that this is part of what it means to live the life of a follower of Christ.

Whenever a Christian prays, it is an essential part of the life of the parish. It is a sign of the presence of the Holy Spirit. Pope John Paul wrote that whenever a person prays, 'there the Holy Spirit is the living breath of prayer'.

The Eucharist is the summit and source of all this activity. The groups that work in the parish, the families and their joys and sorrows, the involvement of parishioners in the life of society, the individual struggles, successes and concerns, the often unspoken feelings of marginalisation, exclusion and pain – all of these are

---

10. Benedict XVI, Homily during Pastoral Visit to the Parish of St Maximilian Kolbe, Rome, 12 December 2010 (my translation).

part of what we offer and all of these are the contexts to which we hope to return with renewed hope and strength.

There is a lot to be done in enabling the whole congregation to recognise something of that variety and richness. The prayers of the faithful, the newsletter, the notice boards, the parish website and social networking sites are not just ways of sharing information, they are ways of enriching our community's life and our celebration of the liturgy by allowing us to know more fully who we are as a community and what our particular gathering prays for and celebrates.

The community that celebrates the Eucharist is true to itself when it welcomes everyone without considerations of social class, wealth or race. If it does not do so, it not only 'dishonours the poor man', it fails to understand what kind of community it is (cf. Jas 2:1-6).

Clearly the honouring of the poor man is not only a matter of how he is treated in the Church, it is a question of how he is treated in the life of the community. The life of the Church is broader than what happens in official parochial events and liturgical services.

Responding to the Word

Many Christians live out their vocation in the sacrament of marriage. That vocation is lived in all sorts of situations: when husband and wife deepen their relationship with one another; when they pray together whenever they try to enrich their understanding of the Christian vision of marriage, so finely presented in Pope John Paul's 'Theology of the Body';[11] when they do their best for their children. When they try to show God's infinite love reflected in their love for one another and for their children they are playing a vital part in the life of the parish. They are 'the domestic Church', the Church existing in the home.[12]

---

11. John Paul II, Addresses at General Audiences, *Uomo e Donna lo Creò* (Rome: Città Nuova, 1987). See C. West, *The Theology of the Body Explained* (Herefordshire: Gracewing, 2003).
12. *Lumen gentium*, 11.

A particular challenge for Christian witness lies in the new languages of the internet and social networking. The speed of change is disconcerting. With due reservations about the difficulty of authenticating information derived from the internet, it would appear that radio took thirty-eight years to acquire 50 million listeners, television took thirteen years, the internet four years, while Facebook acquired 200 million in less than one year!

The long history of the Church has been a story of the challenge of speaking the Good News in new languages. The missionary – and every member of the Church is a missionary – always has to learn the language of a new culture and time. In Ireland, for instance, the early Christian monks became the successors of the pagan druids and poets; they also absorbed the traditions of Greece and Rome:

> An examination of Columban's works shows reminiscences of Persius, Vergil, Horace, Sallust, Ovid, Juvenal and of the Christian poets Juvenus, Prudentius and Ausonius.[13]

Aquinas engaged with Arab philosophy and Matteo Ricci with the culture of China. Today's challenge for the Church is to engage with a new culture and language at least as unfamiliar as any previous missionary context.

In many places, parents, priests and the whole community feel a great concern about how to involve young people in the life of the Church. Young people, on the other hand, feel that the parish and Church organisations do not meet their needs and are out of touch with their world. These two concerns are two sides of the same reality; what they ask of us is clear.

Among that young generation of Christians there must be potential new missionaries who, perhaps without ever leaving their countries, can recognise this new continent, a restless, lost

---

13. John Ryan, *Irish Monasticism, Origins and Early Development* (Dublin: Talbot Press, 1931), p. 381.

continent, but a continent whose language they speak fluently. It is a world which needs to hear the Good News in its new language. St Patrick returned to Ireland after he heard the 'voice of the Irish' calling him to walk among them.[14] A new generation of Irish Christians has a similar call – to walk among their contemporaries bearing the same message in the unfamiliar language of Facebook and Twitter and whatever as yet unknown vehicles the future will bring. Here is a challenge worthy of their gifts!

A few years ago I asked:

> How many areas, even in the lives of believers, could be described as 'religion-free zones'? What has faith got to do with the fluctuations of the stock market, with the looming energy crisis with house prices, with multinational companies, with new research possibilities, with the information age?[15]

The collapse of the financial markets which followed so soon after that talk suggested that the absence of religious beliefs and values from the stock market and such areas of life may not have been as wise and enlightened as it might have seemed! But the concern is a wider one. There are no 'religion-free zones'. There are no contexts in which people should have to leave their beliefs and values behind them.

There are, of course, people who have no religious beliefs but whose values are admirable. They are every bit as appalled as any religious person at the idea of business without a social conscience.

---

14. Patrick, Confession 23, in Joseph Duffy, *Patrick In His Own Words* (Dublin: Veritas, 2000), p. 17.
15. Donal Murray, 'Religion and the Secular in Contemporary Ireland', in *Tracking the Tiger* (Dublin: Veritas, 2008), pp. 56–74; 57. A talk given at the Céifin Conference. This gathering, inspired and led by Fr Harry Bohan, took place annually from 1998 to 2009 in order to reflect on the changes taking place in Irish society and the values shaping those changes and promoting social, human, family and community values.

Religious Beliefs and Moral Values

Nevertheless the question of the relationship between religious beliefs and moral values has to be addressed. For many people the two are intimately intertwined. This is not because values and priorities in the economic and political sphere could simply be deduced from religious beliefs. In fact, in the political, economic, social, sexual and artistic spheres all human beings are fundamentally on common ground:

> Through loyalty to conscience, Christians are joined to others in the search for truth and for the right solution to so many moral problems which arise both in the life of individuals and from social relationships.[16]

One of the most effective techniques for silencing and marginalising the Christian voice is to label particular views about what is best for society as 'religiously motivated'. It is then possible to declare that, while such views should be respected, they can and should be ignored in public decision making. In Ireland one sometimes hears politicians taking pride in their practice of depositing their beliefs in the cloakroom of the Dáil:

> I do leave my religion behind me and I genuinely mean that. While we all have our beliefs and our own religions, I don't think it should cloud our judgement.[17]

This is a distortion of the issue at stake. It is not the case that the Catholic Church believes that the civil law should coincide with Church teaching. The State is not God. The concept of 'citizen' does not exhaust the whole of what it means to be human. The State exists for limited purposes – limited by the constitution and by natural justice. There are many kinds of immoral attitudes and

---

16. *Gaudium et spes*, 15.
17. Dermot Ahern, quoted in *The Irish Times*, 12 June 2010.

behaviours that the State should not and could not seek to regulate. The State deals with external behaviour. It can and should concern itself with manifestations in word or action of disregard for the rights and dignity of others. Selfish or intolerant thoughts, on the other hand, may be very evil, but the State cannot seek to judge the inner workings of our minds without turning itself into a monster.

This does not mean that there is no faith dimension to the issues that concern the State. There is a faith dimension to everything: for a Christian the Good News sheds light on every aspect of life, every aspect of creation. It does so not by supplying new policies and plans, but by giving a deeper, wider vision of the meaning and dignity of human life. It does not create new rules for recognising that dignity but a new appreciation of the truth that we are, all of us, loved by God. We see other human beings as brothers and sisters not just because we are a single species, but because we are children of the same Father and for all eternity we hope to be at home with one another in our Father's house.

That vision should give to individuals, families and parishes a perspective on the immediacy and the urgency of the issues that confront our brothers and sisters, our society and our world. It is not that the followers of Christ would expect to be able to agree on a detailed economic programme or political priorities:

> Often enough the Christian view of things will itself suggest some specific solution in certain circumstances. Yet it happens rather frequently, and legitimately so, that with equal sincerity some of the faithful will disagree with others on a given matter.[18]

The Catholic Church is not a political party. But the follower of Christ should see God in every event, every responsibility, every opportunity. Nothing is secular in the sense of being of no concern in the life of the Christian and the Christian community.

---

18. *Gaudium et spes*, 43.

The life of the parish is all the efforts and all the prayers and all the commitment of all the parishioners in all of these areas of activity. That is what is gathered up in the Sunday liturgy to be offered with Christ to the Father. That is what receives its strength and vitality from that offering. This is an essential part of the life of the Church and of the parish. Any fruitful renewal of the Church in a secularised world has to find ways of broadening our understanding of the parish to include every sphere in which its members live and work.

The giant fully awake would understand that the Gospel is to be lived in every area of life, not as an exercise of power, prestige or prosperity but as a service to the truth and as a source of spiritual energy. There have been and always will be failures and half-heartedness and scandals, but it would be a fundamental betrayal of the needs of today to live as if the Good News had nothing to say, no hope or inspiration to offer to a world that so badly needs it. St Paul calls on the sleeping giant in words he first addressed to the Romans: 'Besides this, you know what time it is, how it is now the moment for you to wake from sleep. For salvation is nearer to us now than when we became believers' (Rom 13:11; NRSV).

Prayer for the Awakening of the Sleeping Giant

God, our Father, you have called us to be your people:

a royal people, to seek and to do your will so that through us your kingdom may come on earth;

a prophetic people, to listen to your word and to speak it in our lives so that your loving, creative word may speak in us and through us;

a priestly people, to offer our whole lives in praise and thanksgiving to you, so that your name may be hallowed.

Help us, Father, to understand that we are your children.

You sent your Son Jesus Christ to lead us to you:

by following him in loving God and neighbour, so that in our lives, our families and our communities we may give ourselves to one another as he gave himself to us;

by walking the path he walked through suffering and death, so that we may always believe in the love which is stronger than every fault, every fear, every failure, every frustration;

by growing in our belief that he is leading us into your glorious life where death and mourning are no more and all things are made new (Rev 21:4,5), so that we may be signs of hope to one another and to the world.

Draw us to you, Father, in the footsteps of Christ, the Way.

You sent the Holy Spirit into our hearts to fill us with all the gifts we need to be the continuing presence of Christ's body in the world so that we may:

 seek out in our communities those gifts that are waiting to be recognised, valued and called forth;

produce the fruits that will show us to be a community united in love, joy, peace, patience, kindness, goodness, faithfulness, gentleness and self-control (Gal 5:22-23);

open ourselves to the Spirit who heals divisions, sets hearts on fire, calls us beyond our comfort and our expectations into the ever new life of God and renews the face of the earth (Ps 104:30);

recognise the Spirit who prays within us with sighs too deep for words (Rom 8:26), enabling us to call you Abba, Father (Gal 4:6).

Lead us by your Spirit into the life where we shall see you as you really are.

We were baptised into the Church in the name of the most holy Trinity; strengthen us:

through our listening to the Good News and the guidance of
the Holy Spirit, to fulfil Christ's command to share the
Gospel with the whole world;

through our celebration of the sacraments, to grow in union
with your Son and in openness to the Spirit;

through the life that is your gift, and the prayers of all your
people, to be true to the gifts your Spirit has given us.

*We make our prayer through Christ your Son in the unity of the
Holy Spirit.*

Amen.

CHAPTER FIVE

Not Power But Love

[...] They eat
their daily bread, and draw the breath of heaven
without or thought or thanks; heaven's roof to them
is but a painted ceiling hung with lamps,
no more, that lights them to their purposes.
They wander 'loose about', they nothing see,
themselves except, and creatures like themselves,
short-liv'd, short-sighted, impotent to save.
So on their dissolute spirits, soon or late,
destruction cometh 'like an armed man',
or like a dream of murder in the night,
withering their mortal faculties, and breaking
the bones of all their pride.[1]

The Mystery at the Heart of Culture
It is worth reflecting on Pope John Paul's words about the
foundation of every culture:

> At the heart of every culture lies the attitude man takes to the
> greatest mystery: the mystery of God. Different cultures are
> basically different ways of facing the question of the meaning

---

1. Charles Lamb, 'Living Without God', 1799: http://www.readbookonline.net/
readOnLine/35083/ [accessed 12 February 2011].

of personal existence. When this question is eliminated, the culture and moral life of nations are corrupted.[2]

So the culture in which we live expresses something about our attitude to the fundamental events of life, such as birth, love, work and death; it expresses something about what we believe to be the meaning of the life we share, about what makes life worthwhile.

One of the basic issues facing any attempt to renew the Church in our day is that our culture seems not to have any integrated attitude to 'the greatest mystery'. Such questions are not seen as belonging to, still less as being the foundation of, a shared culture; they are seen as private convictions which do not belong in the public sphere and cannot therefore be the basis of a shared vision.

It has been said that secularism spreads itself by the ingenious method of assuming that its position is obvious to all right-thinking people. That is a kind of parody of the American Declaration of Independence, 'we hold these truths to be self-evident'. The truths referred to in the declaration, however, are about the equality in which human beings are created and the rights with which we are endowed by our Creator. The secularist approach, by contrast, presumes it to be self-evident that truths about our relationship with God have no place in public debate.

One of the great questions of our time is to find a way in which political, social and economic concerns may become 'reattached' to the mystery at the heart of culture. In other words, these issues need to be seen in the light of people's most fundamental convictions about the meaning of their lives and what is fundamentally important to them. What is at issue is not just reattachment, but a rediscovery of our own depth as individuals and as social beings. By living the political, social, economic dimensions of our lives without reference to who we are and the meaning of our lives, we empty them of their deepest truth.

---

2. John Paul II, *Centesimus annus*, 24.

If faith has no place in politics, these two spheres are detached from one another. If that were so, society would be saying to its citizens, 'your deepest convictions have no place in political, social, economic life'. It would be saying that the State, the organs of civil society conduct their business precisely on the basis that it has nothing to do with the overall purpose and meaning of our lives.

The consequences follow logically. Citizens will know that they are not expected to engage with their whole selves in these processes; they will know that politicians and public servants are not expected to engage with their whole selves and are likely to regard fundamental questions about the purpose of human life as irrelevant. It will be understandable if parliamentary debates are then seen as theatre and elections as show business; they will not have the urgency and immediacy of a real-life engagement with issues that grow out of our deepest goals and convictions. The process will be seen as remote and unreal. Lack of involvement by citizens will be the likely outcome. Is there something familiar about this scenario?

As believers, as citizens, as politicians, as people we need to reflect on how a rediscovery of depth can take place in our culture. What does a Christian understanding of the nature and meaning of human life have to offer in the political arena? It will not be the source of a particular political programme; it operates on a different level. That is not to say, of course, that individual Christians and groups of Christians should not play their full part in the 'political battle'. The role of the Church, as Church, is different. It is twofold: it is to open up minds to rational discussion about the demands of the common good – that is, the well-being of each individual and of society as a whole; it is also 'to awaken the spiritual energy without which justice [...] cannot prevail and prosper'.[3] The believer can never rest satisfied with the plea that nothing effective can be done for a brother or sister. Nor can the believer ever accept that any person or any situation is hopeless. Pope John Paul listed

---

3. *Deus caritas est*, 28.

among the causes of social evils the 'very personal sins' of 'those who take refuge in the supposed impossibility of changing the world'.[4] What is required above all is the moral force that comes from the knowledge that we are loved by God and from the hope that because of that love no effort is lost:

> [The Word of God] assures those who trust in the charity of God that the way of love is open to all and that the effort to establish a universal communion will not be in vain.[5]

The Answer to Human Longings

The goal of human life is not the health of the economy, nor success and affluence; these will always be fragile and can never be enough. Neither is it power and status – which are always vulnerable to those who are more powerful or more ruthless. It is not about building a utopia – which could never be great enough to answer all human longings or to bring final and complete justice for every human being of every generation, living and dead.[6]

The belief in the possibility of an earthly utopia is an attempt to escape from reality:

> They constantly try to escape
> from the darkness outside and within
> by dreaming of systems so perfect that no one will need to be
> good.[7]

Valuable as work for a healthy economy or the best possible society may be, they are not the ultimate goal of human life; they are ways in which people's lives can be enriched and enabled to expand.

---

4. John Paul II, *Reconciliatio et paenitentiae*, 16.

5. *Gaudium et spes*, 38.

6. See *Centesimus annus*, 41, and Congregation for the Doctrine of the Faith, *Instruction on Christian Freedom and Liberation*, 60.

7. T. S. Eliot, extract from 'Choruses from "The Rock" VI': http://www.insidework.net/ static/downloads/products/choruses__from__the__rock.pdf [accessed 12 February 2011].

Here again the temptations in the desert are a crucially relevant lesson – possessions, prestige and power are not the ultimate goal of human existence. Any human achievement is impermanent and every human life is destined for death. We are created for something greater than success or wealth or even the building of an ideal society. If we have lived our lives focused only on these things, we will sooner or later hear the words: 'Fool! This night your soul is required of you; and the things you have prepared, whose will they be?' (Lk 12:20).

Human life finds its fulfilment and meaning in giving oneself to others and ultimately to God. 'Human beings [...] can fully discover their true selves only in sincere self-giving.'[8] For the followers of Christ, the context of this self-giving is that God has first loved us; God's love has been made visible in Jesus Christ:

> In this the love of God has been made manifest among us, that God sent his only Son into the world, so that we might live through him. In this is love, not that we loved God but that he loved us and sent his Son to be the expiation for our sins. (1 Jn 4:9, 10)

Pope Benedict's first encyclical addresses the subject of Christian love. *Deus caritas est* (God is Love) reflects on the fundamental truth on which the Christian life is built: '*We have come to believe in God's love.*'[9]

God's love for us is given freely: he has 'no need of our praise', we can 'add nothing to his greatness'.[10] God's love is a forgiving love, restoring friendship to those who have failed to appreciate, even to those who have betrayed and rejected, the gift they have received. The father of the prodigal son remains a loving father no matter what his wandering son does.

---

8. *Gaudium et spes*, 24.
9. *Deus caritas est*, 1 (italics in original).
10. Preface of Weekdays IV.

God is the absolutely unchangeable source of all that exists; yet, the unique revelation of biblical faith is that God is also 'a lover with all the passion of a true love'.[11] Because we have been loved by God 'with a personal love',[12] self-giving is no mere emptying of ourselves leaving a void, but an opening up of our deepest being to receive the unlimited, utterly reliable love of God.

One of the most important lessons that we need to relearn in a secularised world is that these truths are about the meaning and the 'fundamental decision' of our whole lives. There is no area of life outside this relationship of love; there is nothing in human life that does not find its ultimate meaning and purpose in the personal love of God for us.

Choosing the Way Forward

On the day Pope John Paul came to Limerick, he issued a challenge to us about how that fundamental decision should influence every part of our lives:

> Lay people today are called to a strong Christian commitment, to permeate society with the leaven of the Gospel, for Ireland is at a point of decision in her history. The Irish people have to choose today their way forward. Will it be the transformation of all strata of humanity into a new creation, or the way that many nations have gone, giving excessive importance to economic growth and material possessions, while neglecting the things of the spirit?
> · The way of preferring economic growth and material possessions to the things of the spirit?
> · The way of substituting a new ethic of temporal enjoyment for the law of God?
> · The way of false freedom which is only slavery to decadence?

---

11. *Deus caritas est*, 10: *'veri amoris impetu praeditum'*.
12. Ibid., 9.

· Will it be the way of subjugating the dignity of the human person to the totalitarian domination of the State?
· The way of violent struggle between classes?
· The way of extolling revolution over God?[13]

He reminded us that Jesus had asked his disciples what it would profit them if they gained the whole world, but forfeited their life (Mt 16:26). The Pope then turned the question to us: 'What would it profit Ireland to go the easy way of the world and suffer the loss of her own soul?'

The leaven of the Gospel is the central truth about God's love for us in Christ. The most profound question in relation to any aspect of our existence is how to live as people who have come to believe in that love, how to allow it to become the leaven of our individual and social lives, how to allow it to speak in our lives. That divine love is also the light which darkness cannot overpower. As Pope Benedict said a couple of days before the publication of the encyclical: 'Light and love are the same reality. They are the primordial creative power that moves the universe.' And the wonder of the Gospel, he said, is that, 'God, the infinite Light [...] has a human face and, we may add, a human heart'.[14]

But how are we to permeate society with the leaven of that Good News, with the light of Christ? Many of our fellow citizens do not believe in Christ and many regard any influence of religious belief in political and economic life as an intrusion. What influence should my religious beliefs have on my responsibilities as a citizen? I cannot, and should not, try to impose my beliefs on others; it is equally clear that I may not look on society as a sphere in which the love of God is irrelevant. Pope John Paul in 1979 said that Ireland was at a point of decision. The intervening years have shown how true those words were, not only in the sphere of religious faith but in every sphere of national life. Because of the

---

13. Homily in Limerick, 1 October 1979 (my formatting).
14. Benedict XVI, Address to Cor Unum – The Pontifical Council for Human and Christian Development, 23 January 2006.

choices we made, or failed to make, in the intervening years, the decisions we now face are even more urgent.

The fear of the influence of churches and of people of faith in social and political issues is often linked to the notion that the religious approach will be authoritarian. There are many unfortunate, sometimes deplorable, historical examples of that, but they were a failure to understand the nature of the relationship between faith and society. There were instances when missionaries and others resorted to 'intolerance and even violence in the service of truth'.[15] The Galileo case is more complex than it seems, but clearly the theologians and scripture scholars had closed their minds to what Galileo was discovering. As Pope John Paul said, 'Paradoxically, the sincere believer Galileo showed himself to be more perspicacious on that point than his theological adversaries. As he wrote [...], "If the Scripture cannot err, some of its interpreters and commentators can err in various ways".'[16]

The Church and Christians play their role in the life of society through rational argument, not through coercion. For over three decades the Irish bishops have made it clear that the fact that something is Church teaching is not in itself a reason for putting it into the criminal law; neither is it a reason not to do so. Such questions must be argued on a different basis, the basis of the common good of individuals and of society: the Catholic Church in Ireland 'seeks no power except the power of the Gospel which it preaches and the consciences and convictions of those who freely accept that teaching'.[17]

The issue is not one of 'imposing our religious views on others'. To suggest that the issue of abortion concerns only 'religiously minded people' is a clever but dishonest way to exclude a large part of the population from the discussion. That exclusion can only be done at the expense of our own humanity. It seeks to sideline as 'religious' and therefore 'beside the point' a question that no

---

15. John Paul II, *Tertio millennio ineunte*, 35.
16. John Paul II, Address to the Pontifical Academy of Sciences, 31 October 1992.
17. Irish Catholic Bishops' Delegation to the All-Ireland Forum, 1984.

human being can regard as irrelevant. It dismisses as a 'private' religious question the issue of the respect that we owe to human life in the early stage of its existence — as if it does not concern every human being.

Those, on the other hand, who enter the public arena discussing political issues in the language of the Bible and of Church teaching also misunderstand the situation. They risk reinforcing in others the conviction that these are 'religious matters' irrelevant to citizens who feel in no way bound by the scriptures or by the authority of the Church.

The right to life and other such issues are matters on which the truth is open to believers and to non-believers because it is the truth about our own humanity. The obligation to respect every human life at every stage of its existence from conception to natural death is written into the heart of everyone. We all recognise at some level that a human life is never just a thing to be disposed of as we wish. We can learn this from reflection on the meaning of human life and human relationships, and our responsibility to be true to that meaning. Even the Warnock report of 1984, which gave respectability to experimentation on human embryos, stated:

> Nevertheless we were agreed that the embryo of the human species ought to have special status and that no one should undertake research on human embryos the purposes of which could be achieved by the use of other animals or in some other ways. *The status of the embryo is a matter of fundamental principle which should be enshrined in legislation.*[18]

In light of the Warnock Report and its aftermath it is hard to see what this 'matter of fundamental principle' amounts to in practice.

---

18. *Report of the Committee of Inquiry into Human Fertilisation and Embryology*, 11.17 (London: HMSO, 1984) (my italics). Note the dissenting minority report of Madeleine Carriline, John Marshall and Jean Walker.

It is not the role of the Church to impose its teachings, to exercise coercion as if it were an alternative political or legislative body. That would be a misunderstanding of the nature of the Good News and of who God is:

> It is not power, but love that redeems us! This is God's sign: he himself is love. How often we wish that God would show himself stronger, that he would strike decisively, defeating evil and creating a better world. All ideologies of power justify themselves in exactly this way, they justify the destruction of whatever would stand in the way of progress and the liberation of humanity. We suffer on account of God's patience. And yet, we need his patience. God, who became a lamb, tells us that the world is saved by the Crucified One, not by those who crucified him. The world is redeemed by the patience of God. It is destroyed by the impatience of man.[19]

The Social Doctrine of the Church
But there is another dimension:

> [The Church] has to play her part through rational argument and she has to reawaken the spiritual energy without which justice, which always demands sacrifice, cannot prevail and prosper.[20]

If there is one thing above all that our society needs, it is 'spiritual energy'. Some years ago, Roy Hattersley wrote an article in which he asked himself why, when a natural disaster like a hurricane or an earthquake strikes, the people who rush to help are overwhelmingly believers: 'Notable by their absence,' he said, 'are teams from rationalist societies, free thinkers clubs and atheists' associations [...]' He concludes: 'Men and women who, like me,

---

19. Benedict XVI, Homily at Mass for the Inauguration of his Pontificate, 24 April 2005.
20. *Deus caritas est*, 28a.

cannot accept the miracles and mysteries do not go out with the Salvation Army at night.'[21]

Among those who have no religious belief there are many people of the highest integrity who live with generous commitment to the welfare of other people and to the betterment of society. It is also true, however, that for very many people it is religious faith that prompts them to behave with practical concern and heroic generosity, that inspires them to continue to work for the common good, that gives them hope in difficult or desperate situations. They know that their faith has everything to do with energising and inspiring their life in society.

The challenge is to find ways of encouraging and welcoming that energy without seeming to imply that those who do not believe have nothing to offer.

The Chief Rabbi of Britain Jonathan Sacks sums up the dilemma that Western society is facing:

> For four centuries the West proceeded on the assumption that science, politics and economics would take the place once held by the Church. The problem of religion would be solved by depriving it of power. What happens, though, when religion returns in all its power precisely because it answers questions to which science, politics and economics offer no reply? The great faiths provide meaning and purpose for their adherents. The question is: can they make space for those who are not its adherents, who sing a different song, hear different music, tell a different story? On that question, the fate of the twenty-first century may turn.[22]

The most basic and most obvious step in bringing the Gospel to bear on our society and our world is for believers to reflect on its implications ourselves as individuals and as a community. In the

---

21. Roy Hattersley, opinion piece in *The Guardian*, 12 September 2005.
22. Jonathan Sacks, *The Dignity of Difference* (London: Continuum, 2002), p. 43.

Catholic tradition there is a long history of that kind of reflection expressed in the great papal documents known as 'the social encyclicals', beginning with *Rerum novarum* of Pope Leo XIII in 1891, down to the social encyclicals of Pope John Paul II and Pope Benedict XVI.[23] This tradition of reflection and teaching has become known as the Social Doctrine of the Church.

In fact, all three of Pope Benedict's encyclicals have a clear social dimension.[24] *Deus caritas est* reinforces a point which is sometimes misunderstood. The social doctrine of the Church is not an ideology, not a political programme which the Church seeks to impose; it is rather a guide for Christian behaviour attitudes:

> The Church's social doctrine is [...] the accurate formulation of the results of a careful reflection on the complex realities of human existence, in society and in the international order, in the light of faith and of the Church's tradition. Its main aim is to interpret these realities, determining their conformity with or divergence from the lines of the Gospel teaching on man and his vocation, a vocation which is at once earthly and transcendent; its aim is thus to guide Christian behaviour. It therefore belongs to the field, not of ideology, but of theology and particularly moral theology.[25]

The *Compendium of the Social Doctrine of the Church* gives 'a concise but complete overview of the Church's social teaching'.[26] The words 'teaching' or 'doctrine' might be misunderstood as implying that the Church claims authority over the workings of political society, teaching or instructing legislators about which particular policies are to be adopted. The Church 'does not intervene in

---

23. John Paul II, *Laborem exercens* (1981), *Sollicitudo rei socialis* (1987) and *Centesimus annus* (1991); Benedict XVI, *Caritas in veritate* (2009).

24. *Deus caritas est, Spe salvi, Caritas in veritate*.

25. *Sollicitudo rei socialis*, 41.

26. *Compendium of the Social Doctrine of the Church* (Dublin: Veritas, 2005), p. xxvi.

technical questions with her social doctrine, nor does she propose or establish models of social organisation'.[27] On the contrary, the words 'teaching' and 'doctrine' indicate that the Church is seeking to do something quite different from the State's role.

> [Catholic social doctrine] has no intention of giving the Church power over the State. Even less is it an attempt to impose on those who do not share the faith ways of thinking and modes of conduct proper to faith [...]
>
> It recognises that it is not the Church's responsibility to make this teaching prevail in political life. Rather, the Church wishes to help form consciences in political life and to stimulate greater insight into the authentic requirements of justice as well as greater readiness to act accordingly, even when this might involve conflict with situations of personal interest [...]
>
> The Church cannot and must not take upon herself the political battle to bring about the most just society possible [...] She has to play her part through rational argument and she has to reawaken the spiritual energy without which justice, which always demands sacrifice, cannot prevail and prosper.[28]

Faith does not offer answers to complex economic or social situations, but it does something even more fundamental. It calls us to treat every other human being as a brother or sister who, like us, is totally dependent on the infinitely forgiving love of God, as a person who is called, as we are, to an unlimited broadening of our vision and an overturning of our assumptions and expectations. We are to see every human being without exception as someone with whom we hope to share forever in the life of God in our Father's house. We are never to seek to establish our own

---

27. Ibid., 68.
28. *Deus caritas est*, 28a.

worth by comparing others unfavourably to ourselves. If we really believed that, how would it change our attitude towards and the urgency of our response to the injustices of the world and the suffering of society?

The renewal of the Church in this area is about how members of the Church, primarily lay members, bring their faith to bear on the great issues of social and political life. It is about how each person has a responsibility to ask him or herself how the Good News transforms their understanding of living in every sphere of their lives.

The Good News will not lead everyone to the same policies and proposals, but it will give those who honestly and prayerfully reflect on it a greater clarity and urgency. Taking the Gospel seriously will disturb the complacency that sees injustice and suffering 'from the outside' and acquiesces in the idea that 'nothing can be done until the economy improves' or that 'it will take a couple of generations to solve that problem'. An individual or a community that had reflected seriously on the Gospel would understand what Pope John Paul called 'the gigantic remorse caused by the fact that side by side with wealthy and surfeited people and societies, living in plenty and ruled by consumerism and pleasure, the same human family contains individuals and groups that are suffering from hunger'.[29]

The Gospel brings no precise economic solutions, but it offers to those who contemplate the world in the light of Christ the clarity of vision and the immediacy of recognition that enables and requires the courage never to minimise that gigantic remorse. The Gospel offers no comforting escape, no unrealistic solutions. It calls for an unflinching consideration of the horrors that exist in the world and of the unlimited power of the loving Father in whose hands we are all cradled. Only there lies the truth that sets us free from illusions and opens up the hope which alone is great enough to look our world in the face.

---

29. *Dives in misericordia*, 11.

Lord That I May See

Lord that I may see in your face
the love that moves the universe,
the plan of God hidden for all ages
and now revealed in you,
God's creative Word made flesh.

Lord that I may see your face
in every face,
in every situation,
in every possibility that opens up,
in every suffering and disappointment,
in the creation that is your gift.

Lord that I may see
that, wherever I am,
you are always close;
nowhere is distant from you;
when I fail to recognise your presence
I lose sight of the meaning of my own life;
I go away from you,
forgetting that you have the words of eternal life.

Lord that I may see
that you are the light of God
which darkness cannot overcome,
and which you have revealed
in the love greater than which no one has.
May your light enable me to see
that the deepest meaning of every decision,
every responsibility,
every facet of personal and social life
is to welcome your love for me
and for the whole human family.

Lord that I may see
the hope and the promise that shines from you.
May others recognise in me and in all the followers of Christ
the truth which sets us free from the emptiness we fear
and invites us to the eternal light and love of your Father.
Amen.

CHAPTER SIX

Morality in Crisis

Those who 'live by the flesh' experience God's law as a burden, and indeed as a denial or at least restriction of their own freedom. On the other hand, those who are impelled by love and 'walk by the Spirit', and who desire to serve others, find in God's Law the fundamental and necessary way in which to practise love as something freely chosen and freely lived out. Indeed they feel an interior urge – a genuine 'necessity' and no longer a form of coercion – not to stop at the minimum demands of the Law, but to live them in their 'fullness'.[1]

An Overthrow of Moral Values

If the Church is to be renewed, part of this renewal will have to face up to the way in which we approach moral questions. The question lies much deeper than controversies about abortion, contraception, celibacy and the indissolubility of marriage. What we face in our time is a collapse in the understanding of the very meaning of morality. The collapse is so deep and pervasive that it requires that we think very seriously about what is happening and what it means for our living and sharing of the Good News.

In the Apostolic Exhortation on Reconciliation and Penance, Pope John Paul speaks about the emergence of an ethical system

---

1. John Paul II, *Veritatis splendor*, 18.

'which relativises the moral norm, denying its absolute and unconditional value'. He goes on to say that this approach involves 'a real overthrowing and downfall of moral values'.[2] The theme recurred again and again in his teaching, especially in *Veritatis splendor* and *Evangelium vitae*. And Pope Benedict, in his homily at the Mass before he entered the Conclave that elected him, said: 'We are building a dictatorship of relativism that does not recognise anything as definitive and whose ultimate goal consists solely of one's own ego and desires.'[3] That is strong language.

What does it mean to say that the moral norm is absolute and that relativism is a dictatorship? In some areas of life surely right and wrong must be relative. Aristotle says that it is the mark of the educated person 'to look for precision in each class of things just so far as the nature of the subject admits'.[4] Mathematical accuracy cannot always be arrived at. For instance, one might accept from a politician or an economist a statement that a particular policy has a good chance of succeeding even though the precise outcome remains uncertain. In this area it is rarely possible to be more exact. Only history will be able to assess, and even then historians may not agree, the outcome of policy decisions taken in our time about Iraq, about the challenge of climate change or the financial crisis.

On the other hand, we would expect a minister to be able to answer a specific question about how many full-time employees there are in his or her department.

Sometimes the nature of a subject does not permit absolute judgements because there is no single right answer. The right conclusion may be different for different people. A discussion as to whether custard has a pleasant taste will lead nowhere. For some people it does, for others it does not. It is simply a discussion about people's opinions and, if they disagree, there is little more

---

2. *Reconciliatio et paenitentia*, 18.
3. Joseph Ratzinger, Homily at the Mass for the Election of the Roman Pontiff, 16 April 2008.
4. Aristotle, *Nicomachean Ethics*, trans. by D. Ross, Oxford's World's Classics series (Oxford: Oxford University Press), 1954, 1.3.

to say. However, in other areas we cannot be satisfied with simply noting opinions. If, on asking a pharmacist for advice about a particular ointment or painkiller, you were told, 'Who knows? Your opinion is as valid as mine', you would seek out another pharmacist.

So where does morality come in that spectrum? What sort of certainty is the educated person looking for in moral matters? Is it like the mathematical certainty you expect from an accountant? Is it a well-founded projection such as you expect from someone developing a political programme? Is morality simply a matter of taste or opinion? Is everyone's moral opinion equally valid?

There are many different kinds of moral decisions. Sometimes a decision may have a profound significance for ourselves and for others but there may not be one right answer. For instance, in choosing a partner in marriage, there may not be a 'right and wrong'. Although people in love say, 'You're the only one for me', it is not actually the case that there is only one right person in the whole world that each individual must find if he or she is to make a good marriage. And it is self-evident that the answer will not be the same for everybody. As William James put it, 'Every Jack sees in his own particular Jill charms and perfections to the enchantment of which, we stolid onlookers are stone-cold'.[5]

In making decisions about social issues, people will have differing priorities. Many of these varying views may be based on the same fundamental moral concern for the dignity of people – which is the right and necessary criterion. There is, however, no mathematical formula to determine how the priorities are to be weighed or for working out the exact proportion of public money that should be spent on health care, on education, on housing and on overseas development aid.

At the same time, there would be something very disconcerting about the notion that all moral decisions could be like that. It is a

---

5. William James, 'What Makes Life Significant?', in *Essays on Faith and Morals*, Meridian series (Cleveland: World Publishing Co., 1962), p. 285.

notion which is gaining ground. 'If you sincerely believe it,' people tend to say, 'then it's right for you.'

We all know that there are many areas in which, until a few decades ago, there was a clear moral consensus about what was right and what was wrong. There were moral rules and principles which, it was universally felt, applied to everybody. Many of these now seem to be regarded as merely matters of opinion. Chief Rabbi Jonathan Sacks refers to a phenomenon which he calls 'a profound redrawing of our moral landscape': 'the gradual transformation by which sin becomes immorality, immorality becomes deviance, deviance becomes choice, and all choice becomes legitimate.'[6]

We no longer speak of virtues, he says, but of values: 'and values are tapes we play on the walkman of the mind: any tune we choose so long as it does not disturb others.'[7] But, as he points out, it is not as simple as that.

We are happy enough to conclude a discussion about the taste of custard by saying with a smile that 'There's no accounting for taste'. We do not, however, feel that it would be appropriate for arguments about abortion, the death penalty, honesty in the use of public funds, foxhunting or bullfighting, or violence in pursuit of political ends to conclude in that way. We believe that they are not just matters of taste and we have convictions about them which we believe are true.

Morality is a Kind of Language

Morality is, to a large extent, about how we relate to one another. It is, among other things, a kind of language in which we express our attitude to one another. But if it is to work as a language, both of those involved in the conversation have to be able to understand.

---

6. Jonathan Sacks, *The Persistence of Faith* (London: Weidenfeld and Nicolson, 1991), p. 50.
7. Ibid., p. 41.

When a charge of racism is made against somebody, it is not enough to reply, 'I had no intention of insulting you; my remark was meant to be humorous. Can you not take a joke?' If the other responds and says, 'I don't see the joke; I am insulted', the charge stands. What you say and what I understand both count. I cannot simply dismiss what my words or actions meant to you as being of no account. As Jonathan Sacks puts it, 'A private morality is no more possible than a private language'.[8] A private morality is, to put it in the words of Pope John Paul, 'the overthrowing and downfall of moral values'.[9]

Humpty Dumpty in *Through the Looking Glass* says that, 'When I use a word [...] it means just what I choose it to mean – neither more nor less'.[10] That simply does not work. If you have no way of knowing what I choose the words to mean, then no communication takes place or, worse still, a total misunderstanding occurs. That seems to be what is happening in many spheres. Discussions about moral issues often sound like a disordered orchestra, where some musicians are playing a symphony, others a march, others jazz and others simply tuning up! There is no harmony, no common understanding.

Jonathan Sacks points to the disaster that this can lead to in the area of social life and social responsibility:

> [...] increasingly, governments are unwilling to enact a vision of the common good because – so libertarian thinkers argue – there is little substance we can give to the good we share. We differ too greatly [...] Beyond the freedom to do what we like and can afford, contemporary politics and economics have little to say about the human condition. They give us inadequate guidance in knowing what to do in the face of the random brutalities of fate. We need to recover an older

---

8. Ibid., p. 44.
9. *Reconciliatio et paenitentia*, 18.
10. Lewis Carroll, *Through the Looking Glass*, chap. VI.

tradition – essentially a set of religious traditions – that spoke of human solidarity, of justice and compassion, and of the non-negotiable dignity of individual lives.[11]

We hear constant complaints about lack of leadership, but how can there be leadership without some agreement as to where we want to go? A society facing an economic crisis like ours needs a common vision if it is to follow through the painful steps required to move forward. Individuals and groups are suffering such pain that their instinct will be to shout 'me first!' If vision is lacking, society will be directed by those whose shouts are loudest. A leadership that can chart a just and fruitful path needs to be able to call on a vision that is genuinely ready 'to pursue the happiness and prosperity of the whole nation and of all its parts, cherishing all the children of the nation equally'.[12]

Even on a personal level, in decisions about choosing a career for instance, we would like to think that our choice is a reasonable one. In other words, we like to think that, at least in principle, we could explain to other people why it seemed the right thing to do and to persuade them that the decision we made was reasonable; we might even hope to persuade them that it was correct and that they would have done the same in our place. But here too a common vision is required.

Sincerity Is Not Enough

Because morality is a language, it must be shared. No matter how convinced I am that I am making sense, if no one understands me, I am not communicating. No matter how good I feel about myself and my behaviour, other people may experience it as anything but good. No matter how justified I feel in what I have done, someone else may experience it as an entirely unjustifiable intrusion on them. It makes perfect sense for someone to disagree with my line

---

11. *The Dignity of Difference*, pp. 11, 12.
12. Proclamation of the Irish Republic, 24 April 1916.

of thinking and to say to me, 'I don't for a moment doubt that you sincerely believe that you are doing the right thing, but I am equally convinced that you are violating my rights'. And it is no use responding, 'Well, there's no accounting for taste', or 'That doesn't matter because I feel certain I am right'.

That challenge to my sincere decision does not simply arise when somebody else disagrees with me. It arises every time I look back on something I did in the past and say to myself, 'If only I knew then what I know now, if only I saw things as clearly as I see them now, I would have realised that I had got things entirely wrong'. That is how we learn from experience.

When I try to decide how I should act, I am not just trying to be sincere. I am not just trying to ensure that I feel good about my behaviour. I am sincerely trying to arrive at a conclusion which is true – which respects the rights of others, which respects the truth about the situation, about the people affected by my decision and about myself.

If we are to think in terms of seeking the moral truth, it is necessary to begin by trying to formulate more fully the question we are trying to answer. One question is, 'What is the right thing to do?' That was the question the rich young man asked of Jesus in the Gospel. But he added something; he expressed the reason why he was asking the question: 'What good deed must I do to *possess eternal life*?' (Mt 19:16). That reason is crucial. In his encyclical *Veritatis splendor*, Pope John Paul reflects on the young man's question:

> For the young man, the *question* is not so much about the rules to be followed, but about the full meaning of life.[13]

Pope John Paul says, 'This question is ultimately [...] the echo of a call from God who is the origin and goal of human life'.[14] The

---

13. *Veritatis splendor*, 7 (italics in original).
14. Ibid.

question of how we should live is, at root, a question of how we should respond to the God who made us. It begins by trying to understand the truth about our relationship to God and then to one another, to God's world and indeed to ourselves. In the Apostolic Exhortation *Reconciliation and Penance*, after speaking of the downfall of moral values, he goes on to say that, 'the problem is not so much one of ignorance of Christian ethics but ignorance rather of the meaning, foundation and criteria of the moral attitude'.[15]

Different Approaches

The confusion that exists in much moral discussion today goes back to the question that people think they are asking. Those questions each express a different approach to moral philosophy. Without going into technicalities, the different approaches can be recognised in everyday discussions.

One sort of approach has to be satisfied in the end to say, 'There's no accounting for taste'. For that approach, moral views are an instinctive or gut reaction. If you can get me to see an angle that I had previously not been aware of, that may possibly change my feelings. But even if we are completely agreed about the facts, we may react differently, asking 'who are you to tell me how I should feel?'. That approach is related to a philosophical approach that is based on the supposed impossibility of passing from facts to values. It was claimed by some that facts and values are two completely separate spheres and that one cannot pass from one to the other. In this approach it seems impossible to describe value statements ('one should', 'this is wrong' etc.) as true or false.[16]

The passage from fact to value is made by knowing the *purpose* of whatever you are evaluating. You can gather, for instance, a whole series of facts about a new model of car – its size, its fuel consumption, its road holding, its acceleration, its safety features and so on. In order to pass from these facts to a judgement about

---

15. *Reconciliatio et paenitentia*, 18.
16. See William D. Hudson (ed.), *The Is/Ought Question* (London: Macmillan, 1969).

whether this is a good car, you need to know what a car is meant to be and what it was designed to do. Indeed, until you know that, you don't even know what facts are relevant.

The second approach asks what seems to be a much more objective question. The question looks as though it could be worked out almost mathematically: 'Which line of action will cause the most happiness and the least pain?' It is not as easy as it sounds. To work it out would mean being able to put a precise value on different kinds of happiness – enjoying friendship, music, food or sport; and it would mean being able precisely to compare different kinds of pain – physical suffering, disappointment, loneliness, economic disadvantage, illness and so on. It would mean being able to weigh a particular pain in one person against a particular kind of happiness in another. A terminally ill patient, for instance, might have to try to weigh the level of pain which it might be worth enduring in order to have the benefit of being able to converse in full awareness with his or her family. Obviously, two people in exactly the same situation could quite legitimately reach different conclusions on such a question. Anything like mathematical precision and proof begin to look a very unlikely outcome of the calculation.

There is another, more serious problem. When we reflect, it becomes clear that there is more to a moral decision than minimising pain and increasing happiness. Many kinds of fraud and dishonesty aim at doing precisely that. Alec Guinness told the little old landlady in the film *The Lady Killers* that the vast sum his gang had robbed would do wonders for their happiness and it would mean a scarcely noticeable inconvenience of something less than a farthing (0.01 of a euro) on the insurance premiums for everyone else!

Veritatis splendor points out why this kind of calculation is not enough. Many of the martyrs died precisely because they would not do what seemed to be a minor evil in order to accomplish the good of saving their own lives. They could have thrown a bit of incense on the fire burning before the statue of the emperor and spared their lives for decades of dedicated missionary work. But, the Pope says:

> Martyrdom rejects as false and illusory whatever 'human meaning' one might claim to attribute, even in 'exceptional' conditions, to an act morally evil in itself.[17]

That is because there is more to our actions simply than the consequences they bring about. My actions say something about me, my values, my attitudes to other people and my attitude to God. If what the action says is not the truth, there is no point in claiming that the consequences will, on the whole, be positive. That lie, the Pope goes on to say, violates our own humanity. So there are serious difficulties about an approach which simply weighs up the good and bad consequences without considering what my choice means, what it says about my dignity and about yours.

A third approach is based on authority. People will say, for instance, 'The Bible teaches that X is wrong' or 'If the Pope condemns it, that is good enough for me'. These are perfectly good ways of approaching morality. Only a fool imagines that it is possible to arrive at moral conclusions on every issue independently of one's own tradition and culture. The Bible is a reliable guide and the Holy Spirit guides the Pope and the bishops.

But this cannot be our only way of approaching the matter; one has to go further. Otherwise we would be in danger of suggesting that our moral convictions are unintelligible to anyone who does not believe in the Bible or in the authority of the *Magisterium*. It is possible to speak to those who do not share our faith about why our moral teaching, the wisdom of the Christian, Catholic tradition is in harmony with what it means to be human, that is with their humanity and with ours. Catholic teaching on these matters cannot be dismissed as 'the view of those with religious

---

17. *Veritatis splendor*, 92.

convictions'. It is rather a statement about the implications of human dignity.

It is reasonable and sensible to accept the teaching of those who express the tradition to whom you belong and, in particular, to accept the authoritative teaching of those who are charged with interpreting God's revelation, but that does not dispense us from reflecting on issues and thinking them through and attempting to understand them in ways that can be intelligibly communicated to the world of today.

That is a challenge that each Christian has to take up. Each of us is baptised and sent to help others to see the implications of the amazement at human worth and dignity which Pope John Paul said 'is the Gospel, that is to say: the Good News. It is also called Christianity'.[18] We cannot do so effectively if we do not seriously attempt to understand how that teaching is rooted in the truth about human life.

There are three ways of asking the question about what is the right thing to do: 'What is my instinct or feeling about this action?'; 'What is the likely consequence of this action?'; 'What does the Bible, the Church, or the law say about this action?' It is important to recognise that these are three *different* questions. There is little reason to be confident that people who begin from these three angles will come to the same answer except in fairly straightforward cases. If they do, it will be something of an accident. Any dialogue will in fact be incoherent: the participants seem to be talking about the same thing and applying similar criteria when in fact they are not.

The Deeper Question

The rich young man's question was fuller and more profound than any of the ones we have looked at. It was, as the Pope put it, 'about the full meaning of life'. That is where the search for moral truth begins:

---

18. *Redemptor hominis*, 10.

This is in fact the aspiration at the heart of every human decision and action, the quiet searching and interior prompting which sets freedom in motion.[19]

The question of how we should live is, at root, a question of how we should respond to God. It is the same question, posing the same challenge that is put by the call to 'repent and believe'. Here we come to the deepest meaning of the phrase 'absolute truth' as applied to our moral obligations. There is only one appropriate way of responding to God and that is wholeheartedly, without reservation. God cannot be treated as one person among the many who have claims on me. 'You must love the Lord your God with all your heart, with all your soul, and with all your mind. This is the greatest and the first commandment' (Mt 22:37; NRSV). That kind of love obviously goes beyond what a set of rules, however exhaustive, could lay down. Rules and guidelines can be a helpful minimum, but no relationship of love can survive simply on the basis of the partners offering one another only what they are obliged to give.

Moral living is not simply the observance of rules, it is a response to the freely given love of God who loves us first. That love of God is our hope. God's commandments, the rules of Christian living, 'are linked to a promise', the promise of 'participation in the very life of God':[20]

> The Commandments properly so-called come in the second place: they express the implications of belonging to God through the establishment of the covenant. Moral existence is a *response* to the Lord's loving initiative.[21]

It follows that the search for moral truth is not in the first place about formulating rules. Our response to God is to be

---

19. *Veritatis splendor*, 7.
20. Ibid., 11.
21. *Catechism of the Catholic Church*, 2062 (italics in original).

wholehearted. Our response to our neighbour also needs to go further than 'keeping the rules':

> Love of neighbour springs from a loving heart which, precisely because it loves, is ready to live out the loftiest challenges. Jesus shows that the commandments must not be understood as a minimum limit not to be gone beyond, but rather as a path involving a moral and spiritual journey towards perfection, at the heart of which is love. Thus the commandment, 'You shall not murder' becomes a call to an attentive love which protects and promotes the life of one's neighbour.[22]

Lord, I Love Your Decrees

The other thing that emerges is that moral truth is not something that should be experienced as a constricting burden. Sometimes one is tempted to feel that one would be better off if one was not a Catholic and knew nothing about the rules that the Church lays down. However common and even understandable that approach may be, it looks on the Law of God as if it were some arbitrary imposition. It presumes that it would be no loss to us not to know what God's plan for us was. Jesus came that we might have life more abundantly (Jn 10:10). The glory of God, St Irenaeus said, is the human being fully alive.[23] The moral law is about living fully in the truth which makes us free (Jn 8:32). The more our life is in harmony with God's will for us, the more fully human we are.

For how many people is their membership of Christ's Church seen first of all in terms of rules to be followed? Sometimes one hears people say something like: 'The Church is all about "mickey mouse rules".' How sad that is! Life in the Body of Christ is rather about welcoming God's will — an infinitely wider and deeper concept than obeying rules. St Paul tells us clearly what God's will

---

22. *Veritatis splendor*, 15.
23. Irenaeus, *Adversus Haereses*, 4, 20, 7.

is: 'God has made known to us in all wisdom and insight *the mystery of his will*, according to his purpose which he set forth in Christ as a plan for the fullness of time, to unite all things in him, things in heaven and things on earth' (Eph 1:9, 10). We are talking about the path towards the fulfilment of all that we hope for and infinitely more. What kind of witness do we give to that hope if we respond plaintively like a reluctant child who is told it is time for bed: 'Do I really have to?' It is extraordinary to approach that invitation to travel the road Christ showed us, imagining that we might be better off if we did not know about it! What kind of renewal can we hope to engage in if we seem to regret having heard the Good News?

The longest psalm in the Bible (Ps 118/119) is a hymn of praise to God's will, God's law, which every verse proclaims to be the delight of God's People: 'I delight in the way of your decrees as much as in all riches' (v. 14); 'I run the way of your commandments, for you enlarge my understanding' (v. 32); 'The law of your mouth is better to me than thousands of gold and silver pieces' (v. 72); 'How sweet are your words to my taste, sweeter than honey to my mouth' (v. 103); 'Your decrees are my heritage forever, they are the joy of my heart (v. 111); 'My soul keeps your decrees; I love them exceedingly' (v. 167).

Sometimes people resent the teaching of the Church for 'telling them what to do' or 'condemning' them for stepping out of line. Morality is not some external coercion. The teaching of the Church works, not by force, but by appealing to the conscience of the individual and by the person's recognition of that teaching as true. Furthermore, the fundamental moral obligation is not obedience but love — a love which implies seeking to be in harmony with God's will. Obedience to rules or to any created authority has a place, sometimes a very important place, but it cannot be the overriding virtue:

> An adult who was obedient in his whole manner of living, in all his acts, no matter whether they were connected with

sexual or civic matters, would be unworthy of the name of man. One could consider him only as a being degraded to a state most adequately to be described as infantile. But it is no less clear that in certain special departments of his existence, the adult finds that he also has to obey.[24]

If we genuinely want renewal in the Church there are no shortcuts. We need to reflect and pray in order really to learn that God's will is better than thousands of gold and silver pieces. It is a lesson that we will always be learning, and a lesson to be relearned in each new crisis. Everybody involved whatever their role in the parish or diocese has to be ready to listen – to one another, even to those whose views seem impractical or misguided. Everyone has to learn to listen to the Good News and to the teaching and tradition through which it has come down to us, to the Word of God in the scriptures and the liturgy, to the Holy Spirit. In doing that we may recognise that the first thing we hear is our own opinion, which may need to be corrected and enriched by honest listening.

In speaking to others, including those who do not believe in eternal life, we need to recapture our confidence that every member of the human family is loved and called by God as we are, that the Lord knocks at the door of every human heart and that there can be no contradiction between the Creator's will for human life and what is best for human beings. We ought to be sure that the Christian life, lived wholeheartedly, reveals the light that darkness cannot overcome.

The Truth About Ourselves

The young man's question was about the full meaning of life. That is just another way of talking about morality. To live morally means living life to the full, in the realisation of its meaning and destiny.

---

24. Gabriel Marcel, *Homo Viator*, trans. by Emma Craufurd (New York: Harper Torchbooks, 1962), p. 126.

The most fundamental questions are about who we are and about our relationship to God and neighbour, and our responsibilities to God's creation in which we live. How can we be true to these relationships and to their potential?

In responding, do I recognise God as the meaning of my life, or do I, for instance, try to construct and grasp and hold my own meaning? In responding, do I recognise that the purpose, the highest goal of my freedom is to accept God's gift? In responding sincerely and generously, do I believe that I am becoming more fully what I am called to be and am capable of becoming? Does my response help me to be more fully human, more open to the universal communion into which God calls us?

Do I recognise the other people affected by my decision – or my failure to decide – as being called equally with me to the eternal banquet? Do I recognise them as unique reflections of the God who is my hope? Or do I, perhaps, seek to diminish, ignore or exploit them?

Do I recognise the world in which I live as God's gift to be cherished and cared for? Do I recognise it as a gift to be shared with others, and not just others of this generation?

The question of how we should live is not just about moral rules. It is first of all a question about what human life means, what it is for, where it leads. Perhaps the most fundamental reason why there is so much disagreement about moral issues today is that we have no consensus about those questions. The real issue is that some of the moral approaches at work are not founded on the basic challenge of philosophy, 'Know thyself'. They are the fruit of an 'unexamined life'[25] – a life whose ultimate meaning and purpose have not been thought through in depth. A reflection that asked fundamental questions of philosophical and theological anthropology would not find itself adequately accounted for in a moral approach that does not begin from a serious philosophical,

---

25. 'The life which is unexamined is not worth living', attributed to Socrates in Plato's *Apology*.

indeed metaphysical, understanding of human freedom. It could not be satisfied, for example, with an approach that seeks to evaluate the exercise of human freedom simply in terms of the consequences that our choices produce, and to weigh these consequences in some kind of balance, however sophisticated.

We need to recover an approach that would understand that our choices are more than ways of producing results. They are a language in which we may acknowledge or deny the truth about other people and the truth about ourselves; our choices do not simply produce changes in the external world, 'but, to the extent that they are deliberate choices, they give moral definition to the very person who performs them, determining his profound spiritual traits'.[26] In other words, in our exercise of freedom, we decide not just what we shall do but what we shall be. What we ought to be can only be known in the light of a proper understanding of what it is to be human.

If the moral question has to recognise the full richness of human freedom it has to reflect the full truth about myself and my relationships and to build up the truth and goodness of both. In that perspective, any suggestion that moral reasoning could stop short at feeling good, or producing good results, or even conforming to rules, however wise and enlightened, falls short of that truth.

This is a question of how we understand conscience. It is said that conscience is the primary criterion of morality. There is a sense in which that is true. But there is a deeper question. The then Cardinal Ratzinger posed it in a lecture in the University of Sienna in 1991.[27] How, he asked, do we respond to those who would say that if Hitler and the SS were fully convinced of their cause then they were in some sense acting in a morally good way?

He counters that the moral convictions on which we sometimes act are superficial and do not correspond to the deepest truth within us:

---

26. *Veritatis splendor*, 71.
27. Joseph Ratzinger, '*Elogio della Conscienza*', *Il Sabato*, 16 March 1991, pp. 81–93.

The sense of guilt which breaks a false serenity of conscience, and which could be defined as a protest of conscience against my self-satisfied existence, is just as necessary for the human being as physical pain, acting as a symptom, which permits the recognition of disturbances to the normal functioning of the organism.[28]

When I first read the Second Vatican Council's document on the *Church in the Modern World*, I was puzzled by its description of conscience:

When [people] are drawn to think about their real selves they turn to those deep recesses of their being where God, who probes the heart, awaits them and where they themselves decide their own destiny in the sight of God.

Their conscience is people's most secret core, and their sanctuary. There they are alone with God whose voice echoes in their depths.[29]

This seemed to be speaking of something more fundamental than the voice that whispered that this was right and that was wrong. I now see that it was speaking of the same voice which invites us in the first moment of our existence and to which our whole lives are a response. It is the voice which tells us most fundamentally who we are and what our lives mean.[30]

The various approaches to morality that we have looked at can also be seen as distortions of conscience. The question that our conscience addresses is not just 'what is your gut feeling about this?', 'what line of action will produce the most happiness and the least pain?' or even 'what do the rules or the commandments say?'. All of these are very human questions. They are part of who

---

28. Ibid., p. 85 (my translation).
29. *Gaudium et spes*, 16, 14.
30. See p. 143, paragraph beginning, 'One of the neglected truths of theology is that God directly and immediately creates each individual human soul'.

we are; we cannot avoid asking them — we may learn from them. However, the answer to such questions is the voice of God that echoes in our depths and calls us to decide our own destiny.

That is why the claim that 'I am following my conscience' can never be made lightly. It is not just a claim that I feel good about what I am doing; it is not just a claim that it will make me or others happy; it is not just a claim that I am keeping the rules. It is a claim that, having reflected in my deepest heart, face to face with the One who created me and calls me, I have seen as clearly as I can how, in this particular choice I face, I should live the life to which I am called.

That is where the sin of Hitler lay:

> The fault lies elsewhere, deeper: not in the action of the moment, not in the present judgement of conscience, but in that neglect of my own being, which has rendered me deaf to the voice of truth and its inner promptings. For that reason even the criminals who act with conviction remain guilty. These examples on a large scale should not serve to tranquilise us about ourselves, but rather to reawaken us and make us take seriously the importance of the prayer: 'From hidden faults acquit me'.[31]

The real moral crisis is a crisis about our understanding of who we are and what our Creator and Redeemer has made us capable of becoming. Unless we begin to understand ourselves and our destiny, we cannot begin to understand the moral challenge we face. We cannot begin to face the confusion and the 'overthrowing and downfall of moral values' that surrounds us.

---

31. *'Elogio della Conscienza'* (cf. Ps 18:13, Grail Version).

A Prayer of Gratitude and Freedom
God, our Father, Creator of the universe,
all things were made through your Word.
'We were created in the word
and we live in the word;
we cannot understand ourselves unless we are open to this
dialogue.'

You knew us;
you spoke to us;
you called each of us by name
before you formed us in our mother's womb.
You gave us the gift of freedom
so that we may respond in that dialogue of love.

Our call to live responsibly,
the call to be truly free
is your call to respond with all our heart and soul and might
to the love with which you first loved us.

It is the call to understand ourselves in the light of that love:
to live as people who receive your unlimited love,
to live with love for all those you have loved
and to live in respectful gratitude for the world which is your
gift.

In the depths of the human heart, in our conscience,
we meet you Father and hear the echo of your Word;
there we are alone with you;
there we decide our destiny beneath your eyes.

May every decision and attitude
open us more fully to the gift of your life
where we are destined to be one with you
and with all of our brothers and sisters
in the unity of the Holy Spirit.
Amen.

CHAPTER SEVEN

Built into a Spiritual House

[T]he individual is a living stone of the 'spiritual house' only by remaining bonded to the others and acting with the awareness of this bond, powered by the grace which incorporates him or her into the 'holy nation', the 'priestly community'. The church [...] has for its flesh the network of mutual relationships created between the baptised by the 'spirit of glory which is the Spirit of God'.[1]

Sharing a Way of Life

Christian faith is not meant to be lived in isolation. God chose to call people to share his life 'not as individuals without any bond between them, but rather [by making] them into a people who might acknowledge him and serve him in holiness'.[2] Christian living is inspired by the love of God made visible in Christ and seeks to bring that overflowing love to a fast-changing world. That is not a task for isolated individuals. Bringing the Good News to the world is not just a question of communicating information but of sharing a way of life.

St Paul asks how people could come to believe in him of whom they have never heard. And how are they to hear without a preacher (Rom 10:14)? One might put it this way: 'How are people

---

1. J.-M.-R. Tillard, *Flesh of the Church, Flesh of Christ* (Collegeville: Liturgical Press, 2001), pp. 23—4.
2. *Lumen gentium*, 9.

to believe unless they are drawn by a community in which the message is heard and preached, lived and celebrated?'

That is where and how all of us come to believe. Faith is not an individual achievement; it is not something we could ever have worked out for ourselves. It is a gift of God made visible in Christ and poured into our hearts by the Holy Spirit. It is a gift that no human power could offer. That gift is transmitted to us through parents, family, friends, priests, religious, teachers and the whole community that surrounds us and by the generations that preceded us in the Body of Christ, united in the life and power of the Holy Spirit.

In a society changing as rapidly as ours, these various influences are themselves changing, often dizzyingly. Those who influence our faith, the young people who are called to grow into full and active membership of the faith community, each of us in our daily lives, face new pressures, new opportunities, new expectations and new shocks. In such a scenario things can seem to be falling apart.

Many adults feel disappointment and incomprehension that, in spite of our hopes and prayers, so many of the new generation are not responding in priestly and religious vocations, in religious practice, in involvement in parish activities. We worry about whether the faith of today's children and grandchildren will be strong enough for the new world in which they will have to live. We wonder whether we are witnessing the dropping of the torch which was passed on to us by the generations who lived through hardship, war and famine, not to speak of 'dungeon, fire and sword'.

When things are not working out as we hoped, our immediate response is to blame somebody – and it has to be somebody else! Understandable as that may be, it is part of the problem. It is too easy, and too comfortable, to assume that the fault always lies elsewhere, in the schools, or in the clergy, or in 'the young people of today'.

Each element of the local community and all of the individuals within it have a necessary part to play. Catholic children should arrive at school knowing their basic prayers, having some familiarity with religious practice and religious images, able to speak familiarly about 'Holy God' or 'God our Father', having an awareness of their local church, what happens there and some of the people who attend it. It is depressing, and a sign of what has gone wrong, to hear parents complain that the school is not teaching children their basic prayers – a task that belongs to parents. The teacher who tries to give these children some experience of praying together, an introduction to sacramental life, an understanding of the Church community, should be able to expect that the child will meet a living, recognisable community outside the classroom in the home and in the parish. The parish is not just committees or groups, or even acts of worship. Pope John Paul described what the parish is meant to be:

> The parish remains [...] the pre-eminent place for catechesis. It must rediscover its vocation, which is to be a fraternal and welcoming family home, where those who have been baptised and confirmed become aware of forming the People of God. In that home, the bread of good doctrine and the Eucharistic Bread are broken for them in abundance, in the setting of the one act of worship; from that home they are sent out day by day to their apostolic mission in all the centres of activity of the life of the world.[3]

Aware of Forming the People of God

The most basic step in the renewal of the parish and of the wider Church is for those who have been baptised and confirmed to become aware of ourselves as forming the People of God – and of the greatness of both the gift and the task that this implies.

Every Christian needs to understand this, the most important truth about him or herself: each of us is loved and called by God in our baptism to live as members of Christ's Body. That is the

---

3. John Paul II, *Catechesi tradendae*, 67.

foundation of everything else. St Augustine said, 'I am a bishop for you; I am a Christian with you'.[4] Pope John Paul commented on this dictum: 'On further reflection, *christianus* [Christian] has far greater significance than *episcopus* [bishop] even if the subject is the Bishop of Rome.'[5]

We are, first of all, people who have been baptised into Christ. All baptised people, ordained and lay, are his brothers and sisters. 'They are all members of one and the same Body of Christ, the building up of which is required of everyone.'[6]

The whole community of faith is meant to welcome and encourage those who are being initiated into its life; the whole community has the task of sharing its faith in a way that speaks to the changing world. If young people are not involved as we would wish, the first question we should ask ourselves is whether our faith community, with all its variety of members, is one to which they can hear the power and wisdom of God's Word and in which they feel welcomed and needed. Pope John Paul warned that if the whole community does not carry out that task, the faith will not bear fruit; the process of education in faith will become barren:

> A person who has given adherence to Jesus Christ by faith and is endeavouring to consolidate that faith by catechesis needs to live in communion with those who have taken the same step. *Catechesis runs the risk of becoming barren if no community of faith and Christian life takes the catechumen in at a certain stage of his catechesis.* That is why the ecclesial community at all levels has a twofold responsibility with regard to catechesis: it has the responsibility of providing for the training of its members, *but it also has the responsibility of welcoming them into an environment where they can live as fully as possible what they have learned.*[7]

---

4. Augustine, *Sermon*, 340.1.
5. John Paul II, *Crossing the Threshold of Hope* (London: Jonathan Cape, 1994), p. 14.
6. *Presbyterorum ordinis*, 9.
7. *Catechesi tradendae*, 24 (my italics).

That community of faith involves families, parishes and schools working together. If they are not doing so, particular elements will seek to blame the others – families or parishes blaming the schools; schools blaming the parishes or families; or parishes blaming teachers and families. Here we are in danger of echoing the prayer of the Pharisee rather than recognising that the Christian can find no basis for complacency by focusing on other people's faults. We may and should look to see where our community is failing in its task, but the immediate response cannot be simple finger-pointing. None of us can look at the way in which faith is being eroded in our culture and presume that we are blameless. Nor should we think that if 'they' would only do something about it, all would be well and we could 'go back to normal'.

That would be a failure to understand that the whole community of faith and Christian life has the responsibility to welcome new members and to sustain existing members. It would also be a failure to understand that bringing the Gospel to a new century is not just a matter of getting 'back to normal' but of bringing the Good News to new situations and challenges.

We are baptised in the community and in it we worship God who speaks to us as friends; God came to live among us in his Son, who lives now in his Church. We meet God and we hear his word in the whole life of the Church and its members and in all the overlapping communities which form the Church.

If that does not happen, the young person does not receive a coherent message. What is taught about the message of Christ in school, for instance, may not be reinforced at home or the child may not take part in its celebration in church through all the long months of the summer holidays. Many of us can recall from our schooldays how Latin irregular verbs or geometric theorems disappeared without trace between June and September because they formed no part of our consciousness during that time. It is just as true that young people need to encounter their faith in the 'real world' outside the school. If that does not happen, we need not wonder why they lose sight of it.

Many years ago, I was marginally involved with a piece of research about young people's knowledge of their faith. A couple of thousand young people aged about fifteen or sixteen were asked questions, not about their own faith, but about their knowledge: 'What would you say to someone who wanted to know what Catholics believe about the Blessed Trinity' or the Mass or the Resurrection and so on. The answers were mixed and generally fairly satisfactory. The same students were asked the same questions two years later. Almost without exception the standard of the responses was lower and this was particularly evident in those who had left school since the first survey.

I remember being shocked that people could forget what they had learned about the Blessed Trinity or the Mass. But it was a stark demonstration of the fact that we forget things which do not form part of our everyday experience. No doubt this is even more pronounced thirty years later. The truths of faith can evaporate from people's minds in the same way as we can forget the names of people we have not met for years.

If the gifts of the whole parish and of all its members are not being used, then the parish community is poorer, less true to its message and failing to present the power and love of God as it should. Such a parish – and it is true in various ways even of the best – has to seek the cause of the drifting away of youth first of all in itself and in its members. If, for instance, a second-level school provides a rich liturgical, prayerful, socially involved, responsible context for learning and living the Gospel message, what can be said to a school leaver who asks, 'This vibrant Christian community that I learned about and lived in school, where can I find it now?'

The Church in the Home

In particular it is important to reflect on the role of the family as the foundation of this process. In a good home the infant first experiences being loved, first learns to trust, learns to share. These are the experiences and concepts which will enable the child to begin to relate to our loving God. Building on those experiences, a child learns to pray and to trust in God the Father of us all, to understand the love shown for us by Jesus Christ and to know that God's Spirit is within us:

> In what might be regarded as the domestic church, the parents are the first preachers of the faith for their children by word and example.[8]

Many families struggle through sadness, deprivation, relational difficulties; others are racked with violence and the abuse of drugs; others live in situations of intimidation and loss of hope. Parents and families need support in this responsibility – the support of other families, the support of organisations like ACCORD, which exists to 'promote a deeper understanding of Christian marriage and to offer people the means to safeguard and nourish their marriage and family relationships'.[9]

All of this is part of the light and shade, the joy and suffering of the community of faith:

> There is an urgent energy in our domestic world waiting to be released into the church. The home is a cauldron of emotions, all now charged with the redemptive presence; for that reason it is also a powerhouse of renewal in the church. The passions and prayers, the storms and whispers, the blame and the blessing – all are part of that graced energy. Everything that happens in the unbelievably complex fabric of family life, the light and the dark of it, has God's life-giving heartbeat within it, God's loving signature set to it. And we go to Mass to remember and to celebrate together the extraordinary revelation that no moment is 'merely' human or worldly, but rather a place of grace, every threshold a door to heaven.[10]

---

8. *Lumen gentium*, 11.
9. http://www.accord.ie.
10. Daniel O'Leary, *Already Within* (Dublin: Columba Press, 2007), p. 64.

The family is not just a recipient of care from others. The Second Vatican Council gives the family a crucial and active role:

> This mission of being the primary vital cell of society has been given to the family by God. It will fulfill this mission if it appears as the domestic sanctuary of the Church by reason of the mutual affection of its members and the prayer that they offer to God in common, if the whole family makes itself a part of the liturgical worship of the Church, and if it provides active hospitality and promotes justice and other good works for the service of all the brethren in need.[11]

The document goes on to mention specific areas such as welcoming strangers, assistance in the operation of schools, marriage preparation, support for couples in difficulties, fostering of children, help for the elderly etc.

The Faith of the Young

One often hears concerned adults lamenting the apparent absence of young people from Church life and practice. (This lament often seems to take no account of the absence of so many from the speakers' own age group and how that may affect the young.) The opening up of the message of Christ for young people is a real challenge. It is a challenge that has to be addressed to home, parish and school, not to any one of them in isolation. At a gathering of priests some years ago, the few days of reflection echoed with a challenge posed by a preacher, a challenge with which he, and his listeners, were all too familiar: 'What about the youth, Father?'

That question reveals our vulnerability and our weakness before the situation we face. Parents, priests, teachers and the community experience the sadness of seeing their children drift away from things from which adults drew — and for the most part continue to draw — life, strength and hope.

---

11. Second Vatican Council, *Apostolicam Actuositatem* – Decree on the Apostolate of the Laity, 11.

The situation is not as bleak as it looks. In very many cases the faith of young people is, as the Lord said of the synagogue leader's daughter, 'not dead but sleeping' (Mt 9:24). At World Youth Day celebrations over the last decade, in Rome, Toronto, Cologne and Sydney, I was struck by something quite unexpected. One would have thought that to gather a million or more young people in one place, not for a rock concert, but for reflection, talks, hymns, liturgies, Stations of the Cross, an open-air night vigil and so on, would have been a recipe for sullen boredom – perhaps even violence, drunkenness and drugs before the week was out. That was not what happened. Some years ago, I wrote this reflection on what did happen and on its significance:

> One might imagine that it would be a restraining, inhibiting and rather dull context. Those who have been there will remember, on the contrary, a joyful, enthusiastic, exuberant gathering. These young people are *liberated*. They are liberated to be what their societies do not expect or encourage or allow them to be. They are liberated to think about the fundamental questions of their lives, their attitude to 'the greatest mystery'.
>
> They have grown up in the first generation in history which believed that the task of building a more human society could be undertaken without reflection on the meaning and purpose of human life and without reference to 'the greatest mystery: the mystery of God'.[12] They have left behind them for a few days that culture of shallowness and they feel liberated to be themselves in a way that would seem impossible at home.[13]

The problem remains: for the first time in many centuries we face the prospect of dramatic failure in our responsibility of passing on the faith to those who are coming after us. The first temptation

---

12. *Centesimus annus*, 24.
13. Donal Murray, *Never Alone*, Lenten Pastoral, Diocese of Limerick, 2007.

is to blame everybody else, the second is to engage in panic-stricken activities as if the power of the Good News and the grace of God were nowhere in the picture.

We need to begin with a renewal of our own living of the Gospel. It is not simply a matter of persuading young people, or indeed older people, to engage in the activities of the parish. Mark Yaconelli is a Presbyterian engaged in youth ministry in Oregon. After some years he began to realise the emptiness of a youth ministry which looked no further than keeping young people coming to the club or meeting and keeping them occupied and active while they were there. His judgement on the futility of such an approach is bleak:

> Ministry programmes that respond to the anxiety of adults and/or youth are incapable of awakening kids to the freedom of God. Rather than trusting in the presence of God, these reactive ministries put their faith in attendance, conversions and confirmation class sizes [...]
>
> If the ministry is uninteresting or provides few social opportunities, the young people will eventually leave. If the ministry provides youth with fun outings and occasions to socialise with friends, the young people are happy to play along – provided the ministry is entertaining, the youth are happy to ease the fears of the congregation. They assent to being paraded in front of congregations ('Don't worry, the church isn't dying!'); doted over by congregational leaders ('No fear! Your financial allocations are producing results!'); photographed for the church newsletter ('Have no doubts, Christianity is alive and well!') [...] Just don't expect them to be around when they leave high school – or when the programme budget dries up. Then they'll have to get on with the real stuff of life.[14]

---

14. Mark Yaconelli, *Contemplative Youth Ministry* (London: SPCK, 2006), pp. 24, 25.

A Community that Listens to the Gospel

There would be no point in setting out to renew the Church or the parish without beginning with the basics. Not just at the beginning, but all through every undertaking, there needs to be a focus on what the church, the parish, the domestic church and the diocese is meant to be. It is first of all a community of those who listen to the Good News and have received it as the meaning of their lives. It is a place where we constantly try to listen to the Word of God, where we try to encourage, inspire, guide, comfort and forgive one another in our living of that reality and where we celebrate that truth. The Church at any level is not, in the first place, about efficient administration, whether this is measured in attendance, conversions, building programmes or impressive pastoral plans. All of that is important and needs to be constantly reviewed, not to make it more administratively efficient but to make it as supportive, and challenging, as it can be in enabling the community to 'become aware of forming the People of God' and carrying out the mission of bringing the Word into every aspect of life.[15]

The Gospel message is not ours; the plans are not ours; the successes are not ours, though we must work for them with all our heart and soul and might. In the end, our hope is that all our perfectness will be blessed with ruin and with transformation into something we never envisaged. We must be aware that we are part of something bigger than ourselves, something bigger than the whole human race. That is what is said by Pope John Paul when he spoke of the parish as a setting in which people become aware of forming the People of God. It is also said in the words with which this chapter began:

> [T]he individual is a living stone of the 'spiritual house' only by remaining bonded to the others *and acting with the awareness of this bond, powered by the grace which incorporates him or her into the 'holy nation', the 'priestly community'*.[16]

---

15. See *Catechesi tradendae*, 67.
16. *Flesh of the Church, Flesh of Christ*, pp. 23–4 (my emphasis).

This means in practice that everything we do should be done in the context of prayer – not as a pious moment before we get down to the real work, but as the very heart of the renewal of the Church. This is not just one box to be ticked among many; it is the meaning of all the boxes. Without the foundation of prayer, the boxes are empty.

An ancient prayer, which is found, freely translated, in the Liturgy of the Hours says:

> Lord, be the beginning and the end of all that we do and say. Prompt our actions with your grace, and complete them with your all-powerful help. Through Christ our Lord.[17]

Prayer is necessary, because without the Lord we can do nothing (cf. Jn 15:5). But it is necessary for another, related reason. We need the humility and the hope that come from being genuinely convinced that the work we are doing is not our own. We need to be convinced that it does not ultimately depend on our wisdom and strength.

Otherwise the gifts of energy and insight that we offer back to the Lord – who first gave them to us – may become weapons to be used against one another. Our human wisdom and strength can be deployed to get the better of those who believe that they have more effective plans than ours.

In order to work together with our different priorities and interests we need the prayerful perspective of the 'contemplative outlook'. That is the necessary setting for the beauty and grandeur of the Gospel of life to be handed on.[18] Constantly, and especially when tensions arise and when decisions have to be made, it is vital to return to that perspective. 'Unless the Lord builds the house, those who build labour in vain' (Ps 127:1).

---

17. Morning Prayer, Monday Week 1. The Latin reads: '*Actiones nostras, quaesumus Domine, aspirando praeveni et adiuvando prosequere: ut cuncta nostra oratio et operatio a te semper incipiat, et per te coepta finiatur. Per Christum Dominum nostrum.*'
18. See *Evangelium vitae*, 83.

A House Built by God

The followers of Christ in a particular parish or area do not always look like living stones built into a spiritual house. The reason for that failure, whatever its symptoms, is always the same. It is a failure to appreciate that the house that is built is not ours but our Father's; the Body to which we belong is Christ; the unity that we share is the presence of the Spirit.

That division of the community deriving from a failure to appreciate who we are and where our strength comes from is not new. St Paul wrote to the Corinthians:

> Each of you says, 'I belong to Paul', or 'I belong to Apollos', or 'I belong to Cephas', or 'I belong to Christ'. Has Christ been divided? Was Paul crucified for you? Or were you baptised in the name of Paul? [...] For Christ did not send me to baptise but to proclaim the gospel, and not with eloquent wisdom so that the cross of Christ might not be emptied of its power. For the message about the cross is foolishness to those who are perishing, but to us who are being saved it is the power of God. (1 Cor 1:12, 13, 17, 18)

Renewal in the Church has to be based on 'the message about the cross', which appears as foolishness to those who look at the Church from outside, trying to repair the building without asking what is meant to happen in it.

We are in the familiar territory of the Good News overturning priorities and opening up new perspectives. The ultimate purpose of life in any human community is not possessions, popularity and power. Such goals can never finally satisfy the infinite yearnings of the human heart. A healthy community may well produce these things, but they are not its purpose. That is true of every human society and culture, but it is the very heart of the Church's life. It is significant that the public mission of Jesus began with a repudiation of the temptation to put anything in the place that belongs to God.

The parish's task of becoming what it is meant to be is endless and daunting. It means growing in awareness of being *God's* people, not just a group that exists for itself. That awareness of its identity should shape everything that happens. The task is also to see itself as a people, a family. The mission of letting God's love speak in the community and beyond cannot be carried out by isolated individuals. It is a task for everyone.

To act as a family means trying to understand and to address the issues in the family and in the surrounding society that affect all the members. Every parish faces many such issues. No list could hope to be exhaustive, but we may list some examples:

- how to enrich the understanding of faith and the living of faith and the celebration of faith in the parish;
- how to support individuals and families who are struggling financially or in their relationships or through a sense of alienation from the Church;
- how to ensure that the parish is a place where the younger members feel welcomed, challenged to develop their potential, invited to contribute their ideas and their creativity and their efforts;
- how to prepare the parish to be a living, vibrant society ten years from now in a situation which is largely unknown but in some respects clearly predictable;
- how, without trying to impose an impossible and unwarranted unanimity on political and economic policies, to try to ensure that people in the parish are alert to the issues of justice that surround the parish and exist within it;
- how to address the problem of the responsible use of the gifts of creation and the disproportionate and wasteful consumption of resources that we in the Western world have come to regard as normal.

The parish pastoral council will address some of that agenda. Some of these matters may be dealt with through structures such as a parish liturgy group or youth club. But the variety and extent of the issues point to the need for an approach to renewal which fosters and welcomes diverse and overlapping groups of parishioners. These will be made up of people who share an interest and a willingness to pursue particular areas of the challenge of living as Christians today.

It is obvious that everybody cannot do everything, but everybody should do something. Every Christian has a responsibility to bring the Good News to the world. It cannot now, if it ever could, be assumed that the priests can initiate or be involved in, still less to be the chairperson of, everything that happens in the parish. This kind of activity is already happening in homes and schools and parish groups. In many ways this is the lifeblood of the parish. One important need is to recognise and celebrate these often hidden activities as an essential part of the parish's life.

The renewed parish of the future will have to be one in which this awareness of the varied inventiveness, gifts and potential of parishioners will find expression in many different initiatives. This needs to happen in areas such as those listed above and in many others. It will not be the fruit primarily of new structures. It will grow out of a new sense of urgency and responsibility. The Church of today will have to pray the prayer of Moses when he was asked to damp down the outbreak of spirit-filled activity among the people: 'Would that all the Lord's people were prophets, that the Lord would put his spirit upon them!' (Num 11:29).

If that prayer were fulfilled it would result in a whole network of small groups through which the parish will recognise itself as a 'community of communities'. These groups will be small enough to allow genuine human relationships and sharing from which people will be able to draw strength and mutual support; they will also bring life and vitality to the mission of the parish:

One way of renewing parishes, especially urgent for parishes in large cities, might be to consider the parish as a community of communities and movements. It seems timely therefore to form ecclesial communities and groups of a size that allows for true human relationships.[19]

Prayer of Priestly People

God our Father, Creator of the Universe,
the heavens proclaim your glory;[20]
the earth and all who live in it are yours.[21]
You created the universe out of love
and made us in your own image
to be your beloved children.
May we be transformed by the renewal of our minds,
so that we may present our whole lives as a living sacrifice,
and as spiritual worship acceptable to you.[22]

Lord Jesus Christ, you are 'the true and eternal priest';[23]
in your Body, crucified on the Cross
you offered your life and the whole of creation to your Father.
In Baptism, we have become members of your Body.
In the Eucharist we bring our lives to be joined to your offering.
We offer ourselves and every moment of our lives,
united with your offering on Calvary,
sharing in the completion of your drawing of all creation to yourself.[24]

May our offering become ever more wholehearted;
may we ever more fully understand

---

19. John Paul II, *Ecclesia in America*, 41.
20. Ps 19:1.
21. Ps 24:1.
22. Rom 12:1, 2.
23. Preface of the Holy Eucharist I.
24. Cf. Col 1:24, Jn 12:32.

our call to be a royal priesthood and a holy nation,
our call to be the voice by which, through, with and in you,
creation sings the praise of your Father.

Spirit of the living God,
your presence in our hearts and in the world
continues the priestly work of Christ,
leading us into unity with him in his death and resurrection,
and into unity with one another in him.
The desires of the Spirit in our hearts
are 'exhortations echoing in the night of a new advent',[25]
as we wait in hope for your renewal of the face of the earth.
May we be open to your transforming, life-giving love
which is gathering us 'into the one body of Christ,
a living sacrifice of praise'.[26]

---

25. John Paul II, *Dominum et vivificantem*, 56.
26. Eucharistic Prayer IV.

CHAPTER EIGHT

The Triumph of Mr Gradgrind?

'NOW, what I want is, Facts. Teach these boys and girls nothing but Facts. Facts alone are wanted in life. Plant nothing else, and root out everything else. You can only form the minds of reasoning animals upon Facts: nothing else will ever be of any service to them. This is the principle on which I bring up my own children, and this is the principle on which I bring up these children. Stick to Facts, sir!'[1]

Awash with Information

Today children have access to information and knowledge that would have astounded their counterparts even a few decades ago. When I remember the rather bare walls of my primary school days I wonder at the wealth of information that is on the walls of classrooms today – about botany and geography and meteorology and history and language. Computers and whiteboards open up a world of knowledge that we could not have imagined.

When I was a post-graduate student, people got doctorates for searching out and documenting the places in which an author treated a particular topic and then comparing the different nuances of the treatment. Today the first part of that task may be completed in minutes thanks to a computer search. This is an

---

1. Charles Dickens, *Hard Times*, opening paragraph, spoken by Mr Gradgrind.

enormous resource for those involved in teaching or learning at whatever level in the early twenty-first century.

We see also in these cultural changes the clearest possible indication of the challenge that faces education. We are witnessing the triumph of Mr Gradgrind. At least for the moment, primary education is still centred on the development of the child. In other areas we appear to be in danger of swallowing whole the mantra that 'Facts alone are wanted in life'. To say that *the truth* alone is what is needed would be defensible, but there is more to truth than facts. Poetry, art, joy and sorrow, friendship, hope, mourning, promises of love and fidelity, and moral principles are all expressions of what is truest in us but they are more than statements of fact. Scientific analysis does not lead us into a deeper understanding of their human meaning. The idea that only what is scientifically demonstrated should be regarded as true is not a self-evident proposition, nor is it 'neutral'. It is a statement – not itself scientifically demonstrable – which narrows the range of questions that the human mind and heart may ask about ourselves and our universe. To diminish these aspects of the human search is to diminish human life itself. It would amount to what Pope Benedict called a 'self-limitation of reason' which would try to claim that,

> [...] only the kind of certainty resulting from the interplay of mathematical and empirical elements can be considered scientific [...]

> [...] it is man himself who ends up being reduced, for the specifically human questions about our origin and destiny, the questions raised by religion and ethics, then have no place within the purview of collective reason as defined by 'science' and must thus be relegated to the realm of the subjective.[2]

---

2. Benedict XVI, Address at the University of Regensburg, 12 September 2006.

The challenge that faces education today comes down to this: do we settle for the narrow vision of Mr Gradgrind or do we believe that education is about the development of the human person in the human community? If it is the latter, all education must be founded on some adequate vision of the human person and of the human community.

The Search for Truth

We lament that our society lacks vision. We need to be particularly aware of the dangerous challenge that a lack of vision poses to education at every level. Education is about the search for the truth about ourselves, both as persons and as members of many overlapping communities. It is ultimately about the lifelong search for and gradual discovery of who we are and what our life means. Education is about preparing people for life. It therefore requires an understanding of who a person is, what life means and what is life's destiny.

> Education should address the whole person and every aspect which concerns the integral development of the person: aesthetic, creative, critical, cultural, emotional, intellectual, moral, physical, political, social and spiritual.[3]

Education is the means by which a society engages not only with its young people, but with all its members. It is the search for truth. Such a search is its own justification and does not need any 'ulterior motive'. Education may have many useful consequences, but it does not primarily exist to provide the economy with skills or to develop the capacity for technological research or scientific advance. It exists to enable human persons to grow in understanding of themselves and of the world so that they can become fully rounded persons. This is a lifelong task and even the best school or university can only hope to set its students on that road.

---

3. Donal Murray, *A Special Concern: The Philosophy of Education. A Christian Perspective* (Dublin: Veritas, 1991), p. 19.

What increasingly occurs, however, is that education is governed by Mr Gradgrind, assisted by overcrowded curricula and by examinations which shape everything that happens and which provide distorted criteria to assess the 'success' of the process. These set out to measure principally the assimilation of facts and skills and 'qualifications' rather than the human development of the pupils. The Master of Wellington College, London, describes the situation:

> A liberal education has too often been replaced by an indoctrination of the young in the answers they need to memorise and regurgitate for exams. It is so all pervasive that we simply do not see any longer what has happened, and the education establishment – teachers, academics, administrators and those in the quango penumbra – does not acknowledge the impoverishment rather than the flowering of the lives of our young people.[4]

Questions about the nature of education are also questions about how we understand the human person and how we understand the nature of human society. They are, therefore, central to the issue of the future of Christian faith in our society.

As our education system becomes dominated by the goal of contributing to the economy, as it is judged by criteria of efficiency and finance, as it is focused on preparation for an increasingly fluid job market – all of these having their own importance – is it becoming less true to the goal of educating the whole person of the student? Catholic education especially needs to test itself in the light of what the Dutch bishops said over thirty years ago:

> The furtherance of reverence for creation presupposes [...] that in education, clearly and undepreciatingly, room is made

---

4. Anthony Seldon, 'Our Education System is Collapsing into a Form of Mass Indoctrination', *The Independent*, London, 17 July 2010.

for things that cannot be called directly useful or profitable; disinterested activities will not be looked down on or forgotten [...] A school hinders its pupils from discovering the meaning of life, when the preparation for examinations is its only aim and a large number of passes its only pride.[5]

A Time of Change

The growth of economic pressures, the focus on science and technology, the decline of religious congregations, the growing religious and cultural diversity of Ireland, the creeping notion that, in the end, everything is the State's business, all combine to make this a time when change in the educational scene is highly desirable and is inevitable on many fronts. But it is a time when, even with the best of intentions, disastrous decisions may be made.

It is obvious that, in a changing Ireland, the proportion of schools which are Catholic will diminish. That may be a very good thing, because it will provide alternatives to parents and students who do not wish to be educated in the context of a Catholic community. But there will be a great loss involved if these changes do not take place in a way that allows Catholic schools and colleges to foster their Catholic identity.

The danger is that the tradition of Catholic education may be weakened by society's acceptance of a Gradgrind approach, by the State seeking to impose its own pragmatic philosophy of education or by a failure from within the Church community to appreciate what Catholic education has to offer. This would be a tragedy. Catholic education properly understood and faithfully carried – the ideal is not always achieved – provides a counter-focus to the approach which sees education as having its chief justification in the needs of the economy or of the State rather than in the development of the person of the pupil.

---

5. Bishops of the Netherlands, *On Catholic Education* (Pastoral Letters, No. 9), 11 January 1977.

Why should the Catholic Church and other religious bodies seek to have an involvement in educational provision at all? Chief Rabbi Jonathan Sacks describes education in this way:

> Education is the transmission of a tradition. A civilisation is like an ancient but still magnificent building. Different ages have added new wings here, an altered façade there, rooms have been redecorated, old furniture restored [...] We inherited the house from our parents and we want to leave it in good order to our children. We know that they will adapt it to their needs, indeed we want them to. Nor can we say in advance how they will do so or what the house will look like in the future. But as its temporary guardians, we know that we must teach our children its history.[6]

One of the characteristics of a community is that it has an educational function through which it leads its young members into an appreciation of the traditions and values of the community into which they have been born. This is clearly the case with the Catholic community and other religious communities.

This is more than a question of a golf club passing on its rules, its history and its cabinet of trophies. What marks off a community in the proper sense of the word from a group, an institution or a club is the quality of belonging which it implies. One does not belong to a community simply for a specific purpose – recreational, commercial or the pursuit of some particular interest. One belongs as a whole person and relates to the other members as whole persons.

The Limitations of the State

The State as such is not a community. It is made up of many individuals and groups who work together as citizens to achieve certain political and social goals that are expressed in laws and

---

6. Jonathan Sacks, *The Politics of Hope* (London: Jonathan Cape, 1997), p. 184.

statutory bodies, and economic plans and government policies. But being a citizen is not the whole of who we are. It is very important in modern society, where life has become so complex, to resist the idea of 'the Nanny State', the State that thinks it knows best about, and seeks to control, every aspect of life.

The sense of belonging with the whole of oneself is found in a family, a civilisation or a culture, or, in a particular way, a religious community. When Christians gather for worship, for instance, we recognise that we are mortal, that we are sinful, that our own resources cannot save us from evil and death, that our very existence is a gift of God the Creator and that our hope is in Christ who died so that we might live the life of the new creation. This is a statement about who we are, not just in one or other aspect or sphere of our lives; it is a statement of our whole identity, our very being.

If education is about the development of the whole person, it follows that the primary educator will be the community — and in the first instance the family — to which the child belongs with his or her whole self. It will also, in varying contexts, be the other communities — neighbourhood, religion, culture to which people belong. The role of the State is to facilitate this and to make it possible, not to be an educator in the full sense of that term.

The State as such — as opposed to individual politicians and public servants — does not have a vision of the meaning of human life and personhood. If it sought to develop and implement such a vision it would, especially in a pluralist world, become a tyranny interfering in the religious and philosophical freedom of its citizens. The State may have a role in preparing people to be good citizens, in ensuring that basic skills are learned and so on, but it cannot tell people what they must believe about the great questions of life and death and meaning.

If education is about the formation of the whole person, there can be no real education without a community in which it takes place. An education which would seek to start from a blank sheet, or from a supposed 'neutral' position, would be an illusion. We begin our lives within a tradition which we do not create for ourselves. In that tradition we learn, at first without words, a basic attitude to life. Those who are blessed to live in a good and loving family learn to believe that life has a meaning, that they are valued and loved, and that other people should be treated with fairness, generosity and respect. That tradition, our mother tongue, the experiences which have shaped us as small children, the ability to trust and to relate to others, the capacities and potential we possess and develop, and the goals that attract us, none of these are created by us. We find them in ourselves and in our situation even though we can and do modify them, developing our capacities and skills, refining our motivation and our understanding of the environment and so on, but we cannot behave as though they are not part of the story of who we are. These are the foundations of education and they grow in the context of the family and the surrounding community.

The Formation of the Whole Person

Catholic education is based on the principle that the purpose of education is 'the integral formation of the human person':[7]

> Precisely because the school endeavours to answer the needs of a society characterised by depersonalisation and a mass production mentality which so easily result from scientific and technological developments, it must develop into an authentically formational school [...] it must develop persons who are responsible and inner-directed, capable of choosing freely in conformity with their conscience. This is simply another way of saying that the school is an institution where young people gradually learn to open themselves up to life as it is, and to create in themselves a definite attitude to life as it should be.[8]

7. Congregation for Catholic Education, *Lay Catholics in Schools* (1982), 17.
8. Congregation for Catholic Education, *The Catholic School* (1977), 31.

Catholic education begins with the conviction that the human person is not a series of unconnected compartments. Human life is not a chaotic pursuit of many unrelated and often incompatible goals. It begins with the recognition that our life has a purpose; we have a hope, which is large enough to respond to every question, every longing, every relationship, every suffering, every tragedy and even to death itself. Catholic education believes that:

> This great hope can only be God, who encompasses the whole of reality and who can bestow upon us what we, by ourselves, cannot attain.[9]

Ideally, a Catholic child should be educated in a school where this conviction is, so to speak, 'at home'. If what the child is learning at home about the love of God, about death not being the end, about right and wrong, is not being echoed in the school, if questions about these issues are not being dealt with in a way that is in harmony with or at least respectful of the child's faith, this would be a recipe for confusion. Far from being neutral it would also amount to teaching the child that there is a place – namely the school – where these beliefs are not relevant.

This is particularly important when that faith conviction is no longer 'at home' in the wider society in the way it once was. The expression of religious convictions is often accompanied by a somewhat embarrassed recognition that speaking in such terms may sound eccentric, old-fashioned or out of touch with 'the real world'. That 'real world' poses the question: 'Is it necessary to bring religion, and the differences and separations that this implies, into the schooling of little children? Have we not seen in this country enough of these divisions and their tragic fruit?'

The prevalence of that approach is not surprising. In some cases it may be a reaction to the Troubles and the perception that they were about religion; it is expressed again in the light, or rather

9. *Spe salvi*, 31.

darkness, of the Ryan and Murphy Reports. However, it also reflects an underlying presumption of the culture of many parts of the world, and most particularly of Western Europe. It is presumed that the only 'real' knowledge is that which derives from scientific proof and that everything else is opinion or even superstition. It is said, therefore, that if people want that other kind of knowledge taught to their children, they should do it in the privacy of their homes and not expect society at large to undertake a task that many of their fellow citizens regard as pointless if not harmful.

If we were to accept that as the basis for education, we would be relegating faith to an inferior level of knowledge. We would certainly have travelled a long way from a culture which believed that knowledge of God, however limited and inadequate, was the highest form of human knowledge!

> It may well happen that what is in itself the more certain may seem to us the less certain on account of the weakness of our intelligence, 'which is dazzled by the clearest objects of nature; as the owl is dazzled by the light of the sun' [...]; yet the slenderest knowledge that may be obtained of the highest things is more desirable than the most certain knowledge obtained of lesser things [...][10]

What is at stake here is the human capacity to seek the truth, even to inquire about the ultimate mystery of existence. Granted that the pupils in second class will not be struggling with the higher reaches of metaphysics, but if they are not taught to deal with mystery and to wonder at things that cannot be proved or experimented upon by the scientific method, and if Christian children are not helped to listen to the tradition of faith which

---

10. St Thomas Aquinas, *Summa theologiae*, I q 1, a 5, ad 1. The translation used is *The Summa Theologica of St Thomas Aquinas*, second and revised edition, 1920. Translated by the Fathers of the English Dominican Province. Online edition copyright © 2008 by Kevin Knight.

sees God's presence and God's love everywhere in creation, and Christ as the Saviour of the world, they are not being educated as whole persons.

Secularism and Tolerance

The pastoral letter, *Vision 08*, outlines the importance, in our context, of an atmosphere for education that understands the broadness and openness of the vision of faith and knows that it is not just a particular area of knowledge but the very meaning of our lives:

> In a climate of growing secularism, Catholic schools are distinguished by faith in the transcendent mystery of God as the source of all that exists and as the meaning of human existence. Thus faith is not just the subject matter of particular lessons but forms the foundation of all that we do and the horizon of all that takes place in the school. The Catholic tradition of which the schools are part has been continually enriched through centuries of reflection and development. This not only offers our pupils a rich heritage of wisdom but also gives them stability, a framework of meaning and a sense of direction for their lives in a time of rapid and often confusing cultural and social change.[11]

It is right to acknowledge that such education, respectful and supportive of the faith of Catholic pupils, has been offered down the years in the vocational schools in Ireland. Now, however, vocational schools, Catholic schools, the Department of Education and Skills, the National Council for Curriculum and Assessment, the Higher Education Authority and everyone else involved in education have to face the malign, pervasive influence of Mr Gradgrind. Education, in which religious faith and the questions to which it responds have a central place, can be a powerful bulwark against the sidelining of the deep convictions which are the

---

11. Irish Catholic Bishops' Conference, *Vision 08*, 2008.

foundation for a healthy democracy and are for many people the basis of their convinced and committed participation in society.

At all levels of education this will require courage and clear sightedness. The widening of the base for provision of primary schools will have to respect local feelings. Taking account of the growing variety of views will not be easy. We must be careful not to fall into the shallow and false view that education should simply be 'neutral' in relation to the religious beliefs of the pupils. If God, prayer and religious traditions as lived realities and not just as objects of detached study have no place, this is not neutrality.

The suggestion that religious belief is not relevant to large areas of life is the essence of secularism. It may sound like a recipe for tolerance and harmony – 'let religion keep to its place and we will avoid a lot of divisive issues'. While history has seen many divisions caused and much violence perpetrated by people of strong religious views, this is a distortion of religion. It especially contradicts the Christian vision of a God who wills all people to be saved and to come to the knowledge of the truth (cf. 1 Tim 2:4). An insistence that God is irrelevant to social life is neither tolerant nor neutral. It is a profound misrepresentation of what faith means to the believer. It says, 'God is irrelevant here'. For a person of faith, that cannot be true of any aspect of life.

This is not just a Catholic position. It is very doubtful that Muslim families, for instance, would be happy about a curriculum which has no place for God. So far as possible parents should be free to choose a school in which their religious tradition has its proper place.

Voluntary Secondary Schools

At second level, the challenge may be even more difficult. The number of voluntary secondary schools in Ireland will almost inevitably decrease. Pupils, staffs and parents with years of loyalty to a school will naturally want to do all they can to keep the school in existence. If they see that closure is inevitable, they will look at the possibility of amalgamation, probably with a community college or a vocational school.

Either of these may be the right option in a particular case, but there are downsides. Either closure or amalgamation with a school outside the voluntary sector will diminish the availability of Catholic voluntary schools for Catholic families. The process leading up to such an outcome may well leave the school concerned feeling that it has been abandoned or forced out of existence in the battle for survival by other Catholic schools. It may even be that the school that is forced to close is the Catholic school which has most conscientiously sought to be socially inclusive in its intake of pupils.

There is a bigger picture. The Catholic community, before it is too late, needs to plan for the future provision of Catholic schools. To leave it to market forces and to the 'bloodletting' that could occur as schools fight for survival would not be a worthy witness to why these schools were founded.

It is the whole Catholic community that has the task of communicating to its members, and particularly to its young members, its vision of faith, its vision of the human person in the light of the Gospel. That community task was generously undertaken in the past by religious congregations and laypeople as well as by dioceses in establishing Catholic secondary schools. The decisions that are made in the coming years need to be made in the light of that task of the whole community and in the interests of enabling the whole community to continue to fulfil that duty towards its young members.

The generosity of those who established and ran these schools for so long should not lead us to forget that the task they undertook was not 'theirs' but 'ours'. The whole community is now faced with massive changes in the profile of our educational endeavours at second level. It is a task for all of us, but it needs to be undertaken with the breadth of vision and the courage that inspired those who founded the schools. That means that all of those involved need to come together and to establish as the basis of their cooperation that their overriding priority is not the survival of their individual schools in their present form but the provision of the best possible Catholic education in their areas.

Third Level Catholic Education

There is another area of Catholic education which we are in danger of allowing to slip away. In the middle of the twentieth century Catholic higher education formed a very significant proportion of the total in Ireland: St Patrick's College Maynooth with its Recognised College of the National University; colleges of education – St Patrick's Drumcondra, Mary Immaculate Limerick, Marino, Carysfort, St Angela's Sligo; seminaries – Clonliffe, All Hallows, Carlow, Wexford, Kilkenny, Thurles; and so on. That proportion has now shrunk dramatically with the huge growth of the older universities, the establishment of new universities and institutes of technology, and with the closure of all but one of the seminaries and of several colleges of education.[12]

Most of the Catholic third level colleges that exist derive their academic legitimacy from secular universities or the higher education and training awards council. In many cases these links work extremely well, but they may well prove vulnerable to changing circumstances and changing perceptions of the nature and value of education. The fact that the Catholic colleges are linked to so many different universities and bodies means that they do not form the critical mass that they would if linked to only one or at most two.

The contribution that Catholic education can make at this level is largely unappreciated. Universities are subject not only to the influence of Mr Gradgrind, but also of Oscar Wilde's cynic: 'A man who knows the price of everything and the value of nothing.'[13] Universities are so squeezed for money that any notion that education, the search for truth, is its own justification is beginning to seem hopelessly naïve. What has been said of the United States applies equally here:

---

12. See Peadar Cremin, 'A Catholic Presence in the Higher Education Sector', *The Irish Catholic*, 22 October 2009.
13. Oscar Wilde, *Lady Windermere's Fan*, Act III.

As a nation, we've created a culture that behaves like the Sorcerer's Apprentice [...] — a society where the real organising principle is technological progress in its narrowest sense, and every other social value is subordinated to it.[14]

An apparently small administrative change says a lot. The Programme for Research in Third Level Institutions was instituted to fund research in all areas of third level education: 'research in humanities, science, technology and the social sciences, including business and law'.[15] In 2010 it was decided that the fund would be administered by Science Foundation Ireland, which 'invests in academic researchers and research teams who are most likely to generate new knowledge, leading edge technologies and competitive enterprises in the fields of science and engineering'.[16]

The real value of Catholic third level education is to show that there is something deeper than this prioritisation of technological progress. The purpose of a Catholic university was stated as follows by Pope John Paul, who spent many years, as he put it, 'deeply enriched by the beneficial experience of university life':

Without in any way neglecting the acquisition of useful knowledge, a Catholic University is distinguished by its free search for the whole truth about nature, man and God. The present age is in urgent need of this kind of disinterested service, namely of *proclaiming the meaning of truth*, that fundamental value without which freedom, justice and human dignity are extinguished. By means of a kind of universal humanism a Catholic University is completely dedicated to the research of all aspects of truth in their essential connection with the supreme Truth, who is God.[17]

---

14. C. J. Chaput, Talk at the University of St Thomas, Houston, Texas, 2 March 2010.
15. http://www.hea.ie/en/prtli.
16. http://www.sfi.ie/about.
17. John Paul II, *Ex corde ecclesiae*, 4 (italics in original).

The truth about us and about God is not just information or facts. God is love. Love is not just something God does, it is who God is. The goal of human life cannot be conceived as a thing, a commodity, as something we can acquire or achieve, but only as a gift we receive.

This is true even in human relationships of love; the love of another person never a right to be demanded but a gift to be gratefully received. To treat somebody as a means to any end, however good, is to fail to respect, much less to love them. We human beings are 'the only creatures on earth that God has wanted for their own sake'.[18] This extraordinary statement means that God does not see us as instruments for achieving some goal beyond our own well-being, the full flowering in us of the gift of love which is our destiny.

Catholic education is engaged in a search for this ultimate truth. It is urgent that we give thought to how that tradition can flourish in the Ireland of today.

What we need above all is not better technological research – though that is hugely important. What we need is to become aware as individuals and as a society of who we are. The deepest layer of the human being knows that there is an ultimate truth: 'that at the beginning of all things, there must be not irrationality, but creative Reason – not blind chance, but freedom.'[19]

Prayer to Christ the Teacher
Lord, Jesus Christ,
you are the light who has come into the world,
the way, the truth and the life.
By your words and deeds you taught us to follow you;
you led us to the glory you had with your Father
before the world was made.
You revealed to us the Good News of a world made new.

---

18. *Gaudium et spes*, 24.
19. Benedict XVI, Address at Collège des Bernardins, Paris, 12 September 2008.

Jesus, teacher, you have sent us to the world
as witnesses and teachers of the message you have taught.

Our community and each individual within it
is called to share that Good News,
in homes, in neighbourhoods, in schools and colleges,
in work and in recreation.

We pray for all those who hold particular responsibilities –
parents, teachers and leaders in every walk of life.
We ask forgiveness for the feebleness and distortions
in the witness we have given.
When we do not allow the light to shine through us
we fail all those who could have seen in us
the light and hope of Christ
and we fail the Church whose task it is
to bring the Good News to all creation.

Lord, lead us into the full truth
and help us to witness to that truth in our lives
so that we and others may believe and live the Gospel.
Amen.

CHAPTER NINE

Pray Without Ceasing[1]

When I had come to Ireland I was tending herds every day and I used to pray many times during the day. More and more the love of God and reverence for him came to me. My faith increased and the spirit was stirred up so that in the course of a single day I would say as many as a hundred prayers and almost as many at night. This I did even when I was in the woods and on the mountain. Before dawn I used to be roused up to pray in snow or frost or rain. I never felt the worse for it; nor was I in any way lazy because, as I now realise, the spirit was burning within me.[2]

A Rich Tradition

One of the most welcome, and most practical, reforms of the Second Vatican Council was to permit the celebration of the Eucharist at any time of the day. It made a huge difference to our liturgical practice. It had an unforeseen effect which was not so positive. Apart from the reception of the remains of the dead, occasional celebrations of Rite II of the sacrament of reconciliation and perhaps an annual carol service, it is hard to think of occasions nowadays when people gather in the church without a celebration of the Eucharist. This has led to a reduction in the great variety of

---

1. Cf. 1 Thess 5:16.
2. St Patrick, Confession 16, in *Patrick In His Own Words*, p. 15.

contexts in which we used to pray together. Church services such as sodalities and novenas either disappeared or survived only as part of a celebration of Mass.

While this was understandable, it risked downgrading the use of the many devotions and prayers which were a feature of Catholicism. They were a particular feature of Irish Catholicism, with its prayers for all occasions and its focus on local saints and holy places.

The liturgy of the Eucharist can often be experienced as impersonal, inflexible and full of words. Its signs and symbols are often not valued and understood as they should be, even by celebrants! In most celebrations there is a gap in the area of feelings and of a sense of involvement. Exceptions would be when people gather for a funeral or a wedding. Then we know that we have gathered on an occasion in which we are involved personally, socially, emotionally. In many Sunday liturgies it can be difficult to see ourselves as a group gathered as one and focused on things that deeply concern each of us not only as individuals but as a community. This requires more attention to how we celebrate the liturgy – liturgy groups, involvement of parishioners in ways that highlight the aspects of parish life in which they are involved. But it also calls for renewal of the sense of the parish as a community with a mission to its members and outside its own borders. No truly Christian community can be 'self-contained'. It has to reach out to parishes that have different needs, parishes in other countries, to awakening awareness of issues of justice and peace. The borders of a parish are 'the ends of the earth' (Acts 1:8). Like so many issues of renewal the solutions will not be neat or simple. I believe that the development of pastoral areas can lead to the recognition and blossoming of the many gifts that the Spirit has given so that our community can meet new challenges. These are the gifts, the challenges, the setbacks and the achievements, the hopes and the prayers that the 'priestly people' offer in the Eucharist. That is what they mean by asking the Lord to 'receive us and the sacrifice we offer'.

In past centuries popular devotions of various kinds were able to meet some of the needs for education in faith, contemplation and participation that are a foundation for a richer celebration of the liturgy. They served to root the reality celebrated at Mass in the reality of day-to-day life. An important educational role was also played by popular devotions – some of them, like Adoration of the Blessed Sacrament, closely linked to the liturgy; others, like sodalities and novenas and places of pilgrimage, linked to devotions to Our Lady and the saints. The importance of these traditions was recognised in many places during the Great Jubilee of 2000 when local shrines and feast days were the focus of renewed awareness and celebration. This became a way of recognising the centuries of faith of which we are the heirs. In a world as fast moving as ours, there is a temptation to become absorbed in the present. A sense of the struggles of the past could give a clearer perspective on our present challenges.

It should not be presumed that popular devotions have died out. Knock, Lough Derg, Lourdes, Fatima, World Youth Days, Divine Mercy, Charismatic Renewal, *Lectio divina,* Prayer Groups, Perpetual Adoration, the public recitation of the Rosary, Stations of the Cross, Cemetery Sunday – one could draw up a long list – attract considerable numbers of people. A visit to Knock on any summer Sunday would reveal an active, vibrant culture which is very different from that which many assume to be the culture of 'modern' Ireland. These devotions show considerable vitality and seem to remain surprisingly immune to the decline in religious practice. Perhaps the most striking example of this immunity has been World Youth Day, where millions of young people, not all of them regular Massgoers, participate enthusiastically in traditional devotions such as pilgrimage, the Stations of the Cross, vigils and so on.

Some shrines and associations have made great efforts to integrate a liturgical and theological perspective into their devotions, pilgrimages and celebrations. For several years after the Second Vatican Council, however, they were in some sense 'left behind' by the kind of developments in understanding and the kind of pastoral attention that the liturgy and parish life generally were experiencing.

It is significant that in places like Knock, Lourdes, Fatima and Lough Derg the sacrament of reconciliation is alive and well. People recognise and welcome the proper context for the sacrament; it is an act of worship and praise of God in which we join with the whole community of the Church in expressing our need of God's mercy and our gratitude for it. Receiving the sacrament together with so many other people builds up the sense not just of worship but of a community that worships, receives and celebrates the mercy of God. This is an essential element in the meaning of the sacrament; it should be present even in the case of the individual celebration of the sacrament, with no visible participation of a congregation.

The range of popular piety, from the private recitation of the Rosary and private prayers to great pilgrimages, is vast. It is not just a side issue. This is a powerful way of recognising and responding to God's Good News in a great variety of forms and situations. It is said that St James's Gate, home of the Guinness Brewery, is so called because it was the starting point for the pilgrimage to the shrine of St James (Santiago) in Compostela. This historic pilgrimage has grown in popularity in recent years, attracting believers and non-believers, to share in a journey which in some way expresses their searching.

The Risk of Superstition
The role of the Christian community is to try to ensure that this range of religious expression or searching can in fact lead people to discover and to celebrate the Good News: 'It may never incorporate rites permeated by magic, superstition, animism, vendettas or sexual connotations.'[3]

Superstition should not be too casually or condescendingly identified from some lofty theological height. There are certainly

---

3. Congregation for Divine Worship, *Directory on Popular Piety and the Liturgy* (2001), 12.

examples of superstition around even in our 'sophisticated' world, but the old lady who confidently says that St X will answer her prayer if she recites the novena prayers properly for nine days, will not lose her faith if she does not get what she prays for. Her faith is more sophisticated than her words!

What she brings to her prayer is her need and her trust. With them she touches the heart of the human condition – the longing and the disillusionment, the terror and the light. Patrick Kavanagh saw in Lough Derg 'the banal/Beggary that God heard' – banal because the gap between our aspirations and our reality is found in everyone; beggary because, if we are to attain fulfilment it cannot come from ourselves. He saw it also in a man stretched in craving for something that perhaps he cannot even name:

> A man throws himself prostrate
> And God lies down beside him like a woman
> Consoling the hysteria of her lover
> That sighs his passion emptily:
> 'The next time, love, you shall faint in me.'[4]

That does not mean, however, that the old lady, or the prostrate man, might not benefit by reflecting more explicitly on what they already know implicitly, that they are praying with their Lord: 'My Father, if it is possible, let this cup pass from me. Yet not what I want, but what you want' (Mt 26:39; NRSV).

Superstition and vendettas are not at all impossible in Christian prayer, even liturgical prayer. The purification of our attitudes is always necessary. It is not unknown to hear a 'spontaneous' Prayer of the Faithful which is clearly directed *against* somebody or a prayer which uncomfortably echoes the prayer of the Pharisee giving thanks that one is not like other people![5] It may even be a prayer that is the very opposite of the Pharisee's, while at the same time being no different:

---

4. Extract from 'Lough Derg, in *Collected Poems*, ed. by Antoinette Quinn (Dublin: Allen Lane, 2004).
5. Cf. Lk 18:11.

'For I am tolerant, generous, keep no rules,
    and the age honours me.
Thank God, I am not as these rigid fools,
    even as this Pharisee.'[6]

Popular piety should be permeated by a *biblical, liturgical, ecumenical and anthropological spirit*.[7] The last of these means that popular piety should be influenced by the dialogue between faith and culture of which we are all part — trying to make the unchanging core of the tradition speak to and in the world of today. In the words of a motto that I passed every day when I was a student in Rome: 'Build the new, retain the old, each at home with the other.'[8]

In that process of purification, enrichment and education, as Pope John Paul pointed out, delicacy and gentleness are essential:

> Forms of popular religiosity can sometimes appear to be corrupted by factors that are inconsistent with Catholic doctrine. In such cases, they must be patiently and prudently purified through contacts with those responsible and through careful and respectful catechesis — unless radical inconsistencies call for immediate and decisive measures.[9]

The most fundamental reason why popular devotion can become unfocused is a failure to keep the core of our faith in the centre. There is always the danger of a weakened sense of what is central — namely, the Paschal Mystery of Christ. If that slips into the background then the real significance of other aspects of faith, very important in themselves, such as the Blessed Virgin, the angels or the saints, risk becoming distorted. Their true role is one

---

6. Alice Meynell, extract from 'The New Vainglory': http://poetry.elcore.net/ CatholicPoets/Meynell/Meynell066.html [accessed 12 February 2011].

7. *Directory*, 12.

8. '*Nova erigere, vetera servare, utriusque inter se convenientibus.*'

9. John Paul II, Address to Plenary Meeting of the Congregation for Divine Worship, 21 September 2001, in *Directory*, 5.

of pointing to the core of the mystery, which all healthy spirituality does. The Blessed Virgin's only recorded instruction is 'Do whatever he tells you' (Jn 2:5).

In Lourdes the shrine makes constant efforts to enrich the experience in ways that focus on the core of the mystery. Small changes are made in the Eucharistic processions to help pilgrims be more aware that the whole of life is a journey with the Lord. Each year the pilgrimages have a theme to highlight some aspect of faith. In the recitation of the Rosary a phrase is inserted in the Hail Mary as a reminder that Christ is at the centre – Blessed is the fruit of thy womb, Jesus, 'who was born for us'; 'who sent the Holy Spirit as he promised'; 'who ascended to the Father'.

The second reason is a weakening of a sense of the universal priesthood of all Christians. This, the *Directory* says, 'is often accompanied by the phenomenon of a Liturgy dominated by clerics who also perform the functions not reserved to them and which, in turn, causes the faithful to have recourse to pious exercises through which they feel a sense of becoming active participants'.[10] This is not just a question of ensuring that the congregation and lay ministers say or sing their parts and perform their functions, but of avoiding any sense that the lay members of the congregation are only spectators, however vocal. All of the baptised are actively offering ourselves and our whole lives to God, through, with and in Christ, in the unity of the Holy Spirit. A liturgy which does not encourage the faithful to offer their whole selves with Christ is a very poor liturgy.

The third reason lies in a lack of proper understanding of the signs and symbols of the liturgy, which can lead to 'a sense of being extraneous to the liturgical action'.[11] Any signs and symbols can become dead and empty through routine, through lack of understanding of their origin, through lack of reflection. For the most part in Ireland, the provisions about posture, standing,

---

10. *Directory*, 48.
11. Ibid.

kneeling etc., which help to mark the various parts of the Mass, are ignored. This is a great pity because these are ways in which the 'shape' of the Mass — gathering, listening, praying, being sent out to bring the Good News to the world — is made visible.

When liturgy is badly celebrated, people will turn to popular devotions as something that makes sense to them. What all of this says is that a powerful source of distorted popular piety is a badly understood and badly celebrated liturgy. Popular devotion which is created in response to liturgical and theological poverty will always run the risk of being unhealthy. Popular devotion is not about making up shortcomings in these other areas; it has its own value as an expression of individual and communal piety which complements the liturgy but which, like everything else in the Christian life, sees the liturgy as its source and summit.

Evangelising Popular Piety

The task that faces us might be summed up in the phrase, 'evangelising popular piety'.[12] It is a task with many dimensions. The most fundamental dimension of all is that our prayer and our devotions express our longings, our restlessness, our need for God. There is a great danger that we refuse to face the depth of our needs and the radical inability of anything or any person on earth to satisfy them fully and permanently:

> In the far reaches of the human heart there is a seed of desire and nostalgia for God. The Liturgy of Good Friday recalls this powerfully when, in praying for those who do not believe, we say: 'Almighty and eternal God, you created mankind so that all might long to find you and have peace when you are found.'[13]

All prayer, whether liturgical or private or in an informal group, should do two apparently contradictory things: it should bring

---

12. *Directory*, 66.
13. John Paul II, *Fides et ratio*, 24.

comfort to anxiety and pain by deepening our hope and trust; but it should also intensify our hunger and our longing. Any prayer which dampens down that sense of exile and longing is neglecting its deepest dimension. Aching for God is the starting point of our prayer.

Ronald Rolheiser points out that the first words of Jesus in St John's Gospel are a question to two disciples of John the Baptist: 'What are you looking for?' (1:38). He suggests that the answer to that question is given when the Risen Jesus speaks to Mary Magdalene at the tomb and says, simply: 'Mary!' (20:16). Rolheiser says, 'All of the fire in all of creation, all conscious and unconscious desire, in the end, longs to be so embraced by God, to have God intimately pronounce its name'.[14]

One of the neglected truths of theology is that God directly and immediately creates each individual human soul.[15] We hear that truth mentioned only in the context of the right to life of the unborn child. However, it is of far wider relevance than that. What it means is that, in the first moment of each human life, God already addresses us and invites us into a relationship with him. In his reflection on the Word of God, Pope Benedict says:

> In this vision every man and woman appears as someone to whom the word speaks, challenges and calls to enter this dialogue of love through a free response. Each of us is thus enabled by God to *hear and respond* to his word. We were created in the word and we live in the word; we cannot understand ourselves unless we are open to this dialogue. The word of God discloses the filial and relational nature of human existence.[16]

Rolheiser expresses the same truth:

---

14. Ronald Rolheiser, 'The Evangelisation of Desire', *The Irish Catholic*, 30 January 1997.
15. Pius XII, *Humani generis*, 36.
16. Benedict XVI, *Verbum Domini*, 22 (italics in original).

In the depths of the soul, in that part of us where all that is most precious is kept and nurtured, where we suffer moral loneliness, where we have our purest longings, we know that we have already been touched, caressed and embraced by God [...] There is a place in the soul where we still remember feeling God's embrace and it is there that we gently hear God call our name whenever in this life we meet truth, love, gentleness, forgiveness, justice and innocence.[17]

This is the most fundamental evangelisation of popular piety – to make sure that it does not stop short at anything less than this search for God who loves us since we were first formed in the womb.

There are other elements in this 'evangelisation'. Firstly, the context of all prayer is the dialogue and communion between God and humanity. That is the fundamental meaning of our longings and the only ultimate answer to them. Popular devotions may find their starting point and take their particular character from devotion to the Blessed Virgin or the saints; they may arise out of the traditions of a particular place; they may arise out of some private revelation or some historical event, but, in the end, they should always be a part of that dialogue with God who is love without limit.

Secondly, 'private' devotions are not 'individualistic'; the word 'private' simply means that these prayers are not liturgical rites or ceremonies. No prayer is individualistic; we always pray in the Christian community as members of the Body of Christ. When Pope John Paul said that all pastoral initiatives have to be founded on holiness,[18] he was not talking about what we sometimes call 'piosity', a purely individual relationship with God which seems to find little expression in the rest of a person's life.

Holiness clearly has to do with a person's relationship with God, but that relationship cannot be understood without our

---

17. 'The Evangelisation of Desire'.
18. *Novo millennio ineunte*, 30.

relationship to one another. The idea that we are saved as a people is particularly central to Christianity. We believe that being saved means becoming branches of Christ the vine, and members of his body. The First Letter of Peter calls us to come to the living stone, who is Christ, 'and like living stones be yourselves built into a spiritual house'.

> But the individual is a living stone of the 'spiritual house' (2:5) only by remaining bonded to the others and acting with the awareness of this bond, powered by the grace which incorporates him or her into the 'holy nation', the 'priestly community. The church [...] has for its flesh the network of mutual relationships created between the baptised by the 'spirit of glory which is the Spirit of God' (4:14).[19]

The Pious and the Liberal

Thirdly, prayer leads to action. The danger of individualism is not only that one's prayer is not seen as prayer in the Body of Christ, but also that prayer is not seen as leading to active love of one's brothers and sisters. The German Lutheran scripture scholar Ernst Kasemann once wrote that the trouble with the Church is that the liberals are not pious and the pious are not liberal!

Of course these labels are oversimplifications, but, if we use them as shorthand, and are conscious of their limitations, we can recognise them as describing not so much different kinds of individuals as different tendencies in each of us. Basically we are tempted at certain times to be so concerned about the world and the family, social, political, environmental or economic issues which constantly arise that we forget about God. We are tempted at other times to be so concerned about God in a narrow, individualistic way that we forget about our neighbour and the world. The truth, of course, is that to the extent that we get things out of balance, our understanding both of God and of the world is distorted.

---

19. *Flesh of the Church, Flesh of Christ*, pp. 23–4.

When we pray, whether privately, or in a group on pilgrimage, or in the Eucharist, our prayer ascends to the infinite God whose love descends on us.[20] We are professing our belief that there is a truth deeper than the questions that underlie all human searching and restlessness: 'Does human life, does the universe, make sense?' In the end every human life leads to death; in the end every human relationship ends when 'death does them part'; all human achievements are flawed and every human culture can and does decline. There are no absolute and complete answers in the context of human abilities or human history.

Benedict XVI robustly proclaimed on the day of his inauguration that life does make sense:

> We are not some casual and meaningless product of evolution. Each of us is the result of a thought of God. Each of us is willed, each of us is loved, each of us is necessary.[21]

His first encyclical indicates where the Christian finds the meaning that is both the purpose of human life and the source of its restlessness:

> *We have come to believe in God's love:* in these words the Christian can express the fundamental decision of his life. Being Christian is not the result of an ethical choice or a lofty idea, but the encounter with an event, a person, which gives life a new horizon and a decisive direction.[22]

In his third encyclical, *Caritas in veritate*, he drew out the wider implications of that meaning. After all, the meaning which gives direction, which is the goal of creation, is, Aquinas tells, related to every desire and longing rather as the first mover, the Creator, is

---

20. See *Catechism of the Catholic Church*, 2627.
21. Benedict XVI, Homily at Mass for the Inauguration of his Pontificate, 24 April 2005.
22. *Deus caritas est*, 1 (italics in original).

to all that exists.[23] St Paul speaks of the eager longing of creation groaning in labour pains (Rom 8:19, 23). What we encounter in that 'most secret core and sanctuary' where we 'are alone with God whose voice echoes in [our] depths'[24] is precisely 'the eager longing of creation'. Indeed Aquinas goes so far as to say:

> *All things* desire God as their end, when they desire some good thing, whether this desire be intellectual or sensible, or natural, i.e. without knowledge; because nothing is good and desirable except inasmuch as it participates in the likeness to God.[25]

To our ears, that statement sounds strange – what kind of desire or purpose or meaning can be within things incapable of thought? But that leads us to the heart of the issue. Our present challenge is complex. But one important aspect is that our culture in effect believes that questions about inanimate or non-rational beings are simply a matter for science. Once we accept that, our own eager longing is distorted and we begin to believe that some part of the purpose of creation has nothing to do with our own deepest longing.

Pope Benedict in *Spe salvi* reflected on the new era most clearly expressed by Francis Bacon in the early seventeenth century. Until then, he says:

> [...] the recovery of what [we] had lost through the expulsion from Paradise was expected from faith in Jesus Christ: herein lay 'redemption'. Now, this 'redemption', the restoration of the lost 'Paradise' is no longer expected from faith, but from the newly discovered link between science and praxis. It is not that faith is simply denied; rather it is displaced onto another level – that of purely private and other-worldly affairs

---

23. See Aquinas, *Summa theologiae*, I–II q 1, a 6.
24. *Gaudium et spes*, 16.
25. *Summa theologiae*, I q 44, a 4, ad 3 (my italics).

— and at the same time it becomes somehow irrelevant for the world. This programmatic vision has determined the trajectory of modern times and it also shapes the present-day crisis of faith which is essentially a crisis of Christian hope.[26]

The traditions of private devotion which include holy wells, sacred mountains and places of pilgrimage are not just survivals of a pagan past. The whole universe is totally dependent on its Creator and it finds its whole purpose in him.

In *Caritas in veritate* the Pope pushes forward a unified vision which stresses the inseparability of life ethics and social ethics. Some commentators have been surprised that he refers to *Humanae vitae* and *Evangelium vitae* in this context. But he is saying that the eager longing of creation in the depths of ourselves is an intrinsic part of the longing that is the purpose and meaning of creation. None of the questions of bioethics, for instance, are primarily scientific; they are primarily human and, like every aspect of human life, they concern the eager longing which is the core of being human.

Our relationship to the natural environment is also closely related to this vision, not least because a disordered drive for development has perhaps led us past the point of no return on the road towards ecological disaster. The most fundamental truth is that we, our fellow human beings and our environment, are not just instruments to be used for any purpose we wish. They are gifts of God and their meaning is understood only in relation to God:

> The environment is God's gift to everyone, and in our use of it we have a responsibility towards the poor, towards future generations, and towards humanity as a whole. When nature, including the human being, is viewed as the result of mere chance or evolutionary determinism, our sense of responsibility wanes.[27]

---

26. *Spe salvi*, 17.
27. *Caritas in veritate*, 48.

There are balances to be maintained, of course. It is not true that nature is more important than the human person; but neither is it true that humanity has any right to seek total domination over nature:

> Nature is at our disposal not as 'a heap of scattered refuse', but as a gift of the Creator who has given it an inbuilt order, enabling human beings to draw from it the principles needed in order 'to till it and keep it' (Gen 2:15). [...] the natural environment is more than raw material to be manipulated at our pleasure; it is a wondrous work of the Creator containing a 'grammar' which sets forth ends and criteria for its wise use, not its reckless exploitation.[28]

One important line of seeking that balance is to realise that eager longing for the same final end is constitutive of us human beings and of all creation.

> *Nature expresses a design of love and truth.* It is prior to us, and it has been given to us by God as the setting for our life.[29]

> Truth, and the love which it reveals, cannot be produced: they can only be received as a gift. Their ultimate source is not, and cannot be, mankind, but only God, who is himself Truth and Love. This principle is extremely important for society and for development, since neither can be a purely human product; the vocation to development on the part of individuals and peoples is not based simply on human choice, but is an intrinsic part of a plan that is prior to us and constitutes for all of us a duty to be freely accepted. That which is prior to us and constitutes us — subsistent Love and Truth — shows us what goodness is, and in what our true happiness consists. It shows us the road to true development.[30]

---

28. Ibid.
29. Ibid (italics in original).
30. Ibid., 52.

We might say that when the liberal who is not pious is dominant in us we risk missing the hope that Christian faith can give. One can work tirelessly for social justice, for the developing world, for peace, but it is often a disheartening and losing battle unless one understands that, in Christ, the quest for what is true and good and fully human is never a lost cause. '[Jesus] assures those who trust in the charity of God that the way of love is open to all and that the effort to establish a universal communion will not be in vain.'[31]

When the pious person who is not liberal is dominant in us we risk missing the truth that we are saved not as individuals but as a family and that we will be judged by how we have responded to Christ in the least of his brothers and sisters. To put it at its most gentle, we would fail to allow the fruit of our piety to grow. As St Thomas Aquinas said: 'Even as it is better to enlighten than merely to shine, so is it better to give to others the fruits of one's contemplation than merely to contemplate.'[32] If prayer does not make us more concerned for others, then there is something wrong.

The bitter divisions that can arise between conservatives and progressives, between the pious and the liberal, and between all the various oversimplified labels, are bitter because both sides sense that what is at stake today is the credibility of our Christian witness in a world deaf to the message of the Gospel. Perhaps they fail to realise that one of the greatest necessities for a convincing witness is that each should realise that they have something to learn from the other. The two parts of the one Great Commandment both need to direct our lives. Rolheiser puts it like this:

> If we are to offer any kind of help to a world which is interested neither in social justice nor in contemplation, a

---

31. Benedict XVI, Address on the Occasion of World Mission Sunday 2010, referencing *Gaudium et spes*, 38.
32. *Summa theologiae*, II–II q 88, a 6.

world which, effectively, has written us off, then we had best become liberal and pious, contemplative and socially active, both at once [...] Unless the issues surrounding justice, poverty, war, the ecology, ethnic rights and women's rights are addressed, we won't have a world within which to practise our piety. Conversely if private prayer, private morality, and contemplation die, then we will still somehow lose the world, or, certainly, we will lose any world worth living in.[33]

We need, in other words, to be people rooted in prayer, especially in our liturgical prayer as a community but rooted also in daily life with all its variety and all its pain and all its settings. We need to pray many times a day and in many settings, praying like Patrick 'in the woods or on the mountains', but, like him, we need also to bear the fruits of the Spirit burning within us.

Your Presence Fills the Universe

Lord, we ask you to receive us and the sacrifice we offer at
    your altar.
We bring to you our gifts,
our joys, our sorrows,
our successes and our failures,
our hopes and our fears.
We offer you ourselves,
we offer you the whole of creation.
You are with us in the Eucharist
as the summit of our life,
as the goal of life's journey.

You are with us too as the source of all we are and do.
We are sent out from the church
into a world which is filled with your presence
to recognise you, to praise you and to thank you

---

33. Ronald Rolheiser, *Forgotten Among the Lilies* (London: Spire, 1990), p. 210.

for every person, for every moment, for every place,
for all the signs of that love which we have celebrated in the
    liturgy.

In private prayers,
in holy places, in pilgrimages, in images and processions,
in our Christian traditions and devotions,
in the memory of the saints,
in the heritage we have received from the past
and in all that you have made,
we recognise your presence
and offer to you the gifts that we have received from your
    goodness
and which call us to offer our whole lives to you in the
    Eucharist.
Amen.

CHAPTER TEN

Communion With Christ and With One Another

When we receive you, you transform us into a part of yourself, and faith, hope and charity grow. When we have part in you, the Bread of Life and pledge of glory to come, we the many are one body; then either we eat judgement on our own selfishness or we receive the power of love, which frees, unites and includes everything. When we, as one holy community, raise you up as the sacrifice of the new covenant, when we receive you, then we show your death until you come again, and you renew with us and in us, the mystery of your death. We are baptised into your death. As often as we receive this sacrament we acknowledge your death, which is life.[1]

Communicating the Amazement

In his first encyclical, Pope John Paul spoke of the wonder that we should have at ourselves in the light of the Incarnation and Redemption. He goes on: 'In reality, the name for that deep amazement at human worth and dignity is the Gospel, that is to say, the Good News. It is also called Christianity.'[2] The Church's fundamental function, he says, is to direct people's gaze towards this Good News of what humanity has become in Christ. The

---

1. Karl Rahner, *Prayers for Meditation* (London: Burns and Oates, 1962), p. 50.
2. *Redemptor hominis*, 10.

mission of the Church is to awaken in people the wonder and amazement that was felt by the two disciples of Emmaus when they recognised the Risen Jesus. And they recognised him in the breaking of bread.

So it is appropriate that in his last encyclical he again spoke of 'amazement' – the amazement and gratitude that 'should always fill the Church assembled for the celebration of the Eucharist'.[3] The new vision, the wonder that opened up for the two disciples on the road to Emmaus, is opened up for everyone who shares in the breaking of the Eucharistic Bread. Awareness of the greatness of the divine plan touches our 'deepest sphere' and the whole of our lives.[4] It follows that an essential key to our faithful following of Christ and our faithful passing on of his Good News is that our celebration of the Eucharist should touch us deep in our hearts and should affect every aspect of our lives – the hopes, the pain, the lost-ness and the joys.

An important step in our efforts to carry out the Church's mission and to plan for the future is to 'rekindle our Eucharistic amazement'.[5] The Liturgy of the Word poses that challenge in every Mass. The Word of God is not like a piece of information to be filed away in case it might prove to be the answer in a pub quiz or a crossword; it is not a trite observation about the weather by which we make polite but trivial conversation to pass the time with a stranger. The Word of God is the One through whom all things were made, the Son through whom God finally speaks to us (Heb 1:2). The Word is made flesh in Jesus Christ. 'It is he himself who speaks when the holy scriptures are read in the Church.'[6]

This is a fundamental task for each Christian, to try to listen more attentively and more openly to the Word of God. Each person needs to recognise that he or she has to take a personal responsibility for this. It cannot be a matter of waiting for the

---

3. John Paul II, *Ecclesia de Eucharistia*, 5.
4. See *Redemptor hominis*, 10.
5. See *Ecclesia de Eucharistia*, 6.
6. *Sacrosanctum concilium*, 7.

parish to 'put something on' or waiting until one 'has the time'. Listening to the word is our first and permanent task. It is a task given to us at baptism, when the celebrant touches the ears of the new Christian and says:

> The Lord Jesus made the deaf hear and the dumb speak.
> May he soon touch your ears to receive his word,
> and your mouth to proclaim his faith
> to the praise and glory of God the Father.

The task of the Church, and of each baptised person, is to hear the word and then to speak it to the world of the twenty-first century in a language that is contemporary, challenging and Christian. The role of believers in the creative, artistic field will be crucial as will openness to understand what the artist reveals about our world. To speak the word well one needs to know not only theology but humanity.

It is not enough to repeat the Good News in the words and the style of a previous century. It will have to be spoken by people who have taken up the challenge of understanding what the Gospel says to their lives in all the variety and concreteness of our day. They will then have the task of living that message in a new world in which the Gospel has never been lived before. In the complexity and specialisation of contemporary life, the followers of Christ must speak the Word of God in a way that touches the real questions – and the hearts – of people today. Those who work in finance or industry, for instance, will have to find ways of speaking the Gospel in the technical language of their specialised area, 'a language that the clergy do not know'. The Word of God can and must be spoken in all the languages of humanity – not just national and local languages but languages of science, economics, poetry, information technology, social networking and gaming.

It is the same Gospel that has to be spoken, the same amazement that is recognised in the breaking of bread; the same wonder at God's love for us that characterises us as a community of faith. The Word of God will not give new technical or economic solutions but it will help place various spheres of life and work in the context of the meaning and purpose of life, which is where they ultimately find their own meaning.

Union with Christ the Head

The *Catechism of the Catholic Church* says: 'The principal fruit of receiving the Eucharist in Holy Communion is an intimate union with Christ Jesus.'[7] The Eucharist builds the community of faith — the subject of Pope John Paul's last encyclical. The ultimate fruit of the Eucharist, the *res sacramenti* as it is called, is not the Real Presence, not even the sanctification of the recipient. It is the gathering into unity of the mystical Body of Christ.[8] The Eucharist gathers us into 'communion with Christ and with one another' — the theme of the 2012 Eucharistic Congress. The end purpose of the Eucharist is what one author calls 'the realised mystery':

> [...] the 'realised mystery' is a sanctified people who have become 'one body, one spirit in Christ'. This sanctified people in turn become a *sanctifying* people.[9]

The Mass is the moment of truth when we are most closely in touch with the meaning of life, the common meaning of all of our lives. The Sunday Eucharist is not a stepping aside from life's journey; it is our meeting with Christ, the Way. Our arrival at the goal, while it asks for our best efforts, is, in the end, his gift to us. The end of our journey is to be welcomed by him into our Father's house which is 'not made with hands, that is, not of this creation' (Heb 9:11). Without Jesus, life's journey would not make sense. It is a journey with him to his Father's side. Patrick Kavanagh goes to the heart of it:

---

7. *Catechism of the Catholic Church*, 1391.

8. Aquinas, *Summa theologiae*, III q 73.3.

9. Paul Philibert, *The Priesthood of the Faithful* (Collegeville: Liturgical Press, 2005), p. 65 (italics in original). See also pp. 158–63.

> Don't fear, don't fear, I said to my soul:
> The Bedlam of Time is an empty bucket rattled,
> 'Tis you who will say in the end who best battled.
> Only they who fly home to God have flown at all.[10]

When we celebrate the Eucharist, we are led into a universal unity. We gather around the Body of Christ, we gather in the Body of Christ and we receive the Body of Christ: 'What do those who receive it become? The Body of Christ — not many bodies but one body.'[11]

We pray that we may be filled with the Holy Spirit and 'become one body, one spirit in Christ'.[12] It is a prayer not just for this congregation to live as a community of faith and life, but a prayer which sees us as part of the great family of God's People across all boundaries of space and time. In every Mass we pray for our Pope, for the bishop of the diocese, for all bishops and for the Church throughout the world; we express our unity with Mary, the apostles and the saints who have done God's will throughout the ages.[13]

The celebration of the Eucharist cannot take place without a priest who has been ordained by a bishop who is part of the episcopal succession linking us to the apostles. That is a sign that what we do in the Mass is not just a celebration of the efforts and achievements of this particular congregation. It is the action of Christ, the Head of the Body, in whose name the priest acts. It is a gift going back to the night when Jesus said to his apostles, 'Do this in remembrance of me' (Lk 22:19). This is not something that the congregation could do out of its own resources. It can celebrate the Eucharist only as part of what Pope John Paul called its 'cosmic character':

---

10. Extract from 'Beyond the Headlines', in *Collected Poems*, ed. by Antoinette Quinn (Dublin: Allen Lane, 2004).
11. St John Chrysostom, quoted in *Ecclesia de Eucharistia*, 23.
12. Eucharistic Prayer III.
13. Eucharistic Prayer II.

Because even when it is celebrated on the humble altar of a country church, the Eucharist is always in some way celebrated *on the altar of the world*. It unites heaven and earth. It embraces and permeates all creation.[14]

In using the phrase, 'on the altar of the world', the Pope was surely echoing Teilhard de Chardin's essay 'The Mass on the World', which was composed in a Chinese desert:

Since once again, Lord [...] I have neither bread, nor wine, nor altar, I will raise myself beyond these symbols, up to the pure majesty of the real itself; I, your priest, will make the whole earth my altar and on it will offer you all the labours and sufferings of the world.[15]

The celebration of the Eucharist proclaims us to be the voice of God's creation offering itself in praise to its Creator. We do so as part of a wider Christian community, linked to the whole Church and its history, united to Christ, to all the angels and saints, and to all of creation. We need to rekindle the wonder and amazement of that belonging. The image of the Church that dominates our culture is framed in terms of controversies and scandals, personalities and tensions. It is not that we should ignore the trees — it is hardly possible to ignore them — but we are in danger of losing sight of the wood!

Looking to the future means looking into the unknown. It is true that we cannot know what disasters or joys may lie ahead for our country or for the world. We have no guarantees that the Catholic faith in Ireland will not decline to virtual extinction as it did in other regions, like North Africa, where it was once vibrant. But in the Eucharist we look to a future which is glorious, which is certain and which has already begun. The community gathers

---

14. *Ecclesia de Eucharistia*, 8 (italics in original).
15. Teilhard de Chardin, *Hymn of the Universe* (London: Collins, 1970), p. 19.

in the presence of our crucified and risen Lord, with the apostles and martyrs and all the saints, with all those who have gone before us into the light of God's presence.

With All the Angels and Saints

Pope John Paul on a number of occasions points to aspects of the Eucharist which 'merit(s) greater attention'. One of these is the fact that in the Mass we are united with the great multitude of heaven; the liturgy 'pierces the clouds of our history and lights up our journey'.[16] As we try to build a community that lives and shares the Good News, we are not fighting a losing battle, we are making ourselves ready to be received into the glory that has already begun and that we 'truly glimpse' in the Eucharist. If the building of the new creation were our work, it would be a hopeless task. Because it is God's work, it cannot be defeated. And so the Eucharist 'spurs us on our journey through history and plants a seed of living hope in our daily commitment to the work before us'.[17]

We are also part of a greater community – the whole human family. All sorts of religious and non-religious influences, many different cultures and traditions are part of the air we breathe. This is not something that we should resent or fear. The Good News is meant for all, and we have the privilege and the duty of helping others to recognise the truth of Christ's presence and to recognise the Spirit of Christ at work in them. Every Christian is sent to bring the Good News 'to all nations' (Lk 24:47). All Christian living, by definition, is missionary.[18] Being missionary was from the beginning 'the normal outcome of Christian living, to which every believer was committed'.[19]

In the Eucharist we celebrate and deepen our sense of sharing with one another in the life of God and in the mission of Christ. This sense of belonging and sharing does not 'just happen'.

---

16. *Ecclesia de Eucharistia*, 19.
17. Ibid., 20.
18. Second Vatican Council, *Ad gentes*, 2.
19. Ibid., 27.

It requires proper preparation, serious attention and full participation of mind and heart. Here is another aspect of the Eucharist which Pope John Paul points to as needing greater attention: 'On the pastoral level the community aspect of the Sunday celebration should be particularly stressed.'[20]

Sent Out

A third aspect of the Eucharist which Pope John Paul signalled as needing 'to be better valued and appreciated' is the Prayer after Communion and the Concluding Rite, which should send us out from the Mass with a deeper sense of the responsibility given to us by Christ:

> For the faithful who have understood the meaning of what they have done, the Eucharistic celebration does not stop at the church door. Like the first witnesses of the Resurrection, Christians who gather each Sunday to experience and proclaim the presence of the Risen Lord are called to evangelise and bear witness in their daily lives.[21]

By being united with Christ, the members of Christ's Church become a 'sacrament', in other words an effective sign and instrument of the presence and action of Jesus, the light of the world and the salt of the earth.[22] More than that, by being united with Christ, they share in his priesthood, that is, they share in his role of offering the whole of creation to his Father. In the new creation all human effort and achievement will be found again freed from sin, transfigured into glory.[23] It is our task to offer through our living and through our taking part in the Mass, the parts of creation in which we live and which we have influenced for good or ill.

---

20. John Paul II, *Dies Domini*, 35.
21. Ibid., 45.
22. See *Ecclesia de Eucharistia*, 22.
23. See *Gaudium et spes*, 39.

One of the most crucial elements in a renewal of the Church is an awareness that this mission belongs by baptism to all Christians, who 'are incorporated into Christ, are constituted the people of God [and] have been made sharers in their own way in the priestly, prophetic and kingly office of Christ and play their part in carrying out the mission of the whole Christian people in the church and in the world'.[24]

The list of ways in which we need to reach out is endless and no one individual or parish can do everything, but each can offer his or her life, opportunities, losses and failures to God for blessing and healing. In the Eucharist we find the strength and the motivation to reach out in a whole range of ways.[25]

In a special way we need to reach out to all those brothers and sisters, baptised into Christ's Body, who cannot fully share with us at the Lord's Table:

> It is not yet possible to celebrate together the same Eucharistic Liturgy. And yet we do have a burning desire to join in celebrating the one Eucharist of the Lord, and this desire itself is already a common prayer of praise, a single supplication. Together we speak to the Father and increasingly we do so 'with one heart'.[26]

That burning desire, and our concern for all who are our brothers and sisters in Christ through baptism, should be expressed in the Prayer of the Faithful and throughout the celebration whose goal and ultimate purpose is, as we saw, the unity of Christ's body. If such prayers are offered only during the Week of Prayer for Christian Unity, it would suggest that the desire for unity is not burning as intensely as it should. Every Mass is a prayer for the unity of Christians.

---

24. *Lumen gentium*, 31.
25. See also chap. 7.
26. John Paul II, *Ut unum sint*, 45.

'All are welcome in this place'[27]

In the celebration of the Eucharist, we must be consistent.[28] We cannot both proclaim that the meaning of life and the value of people are not dependent on possessions, status and power and still exclude those who lack these things. If there are those who feel excluded because of poverty, race or social standing, it is a judgement on our celebration.[29] We know that we have an obligation to ensure that 'in every Christian community the poor feel at home. Would not this approach be the greatest and most effective presentation of the good news of the Kingdom?'[30]

If there are those who feel unwelcome or excluded because they are strangers in our community, our lives should reflect to them our realisation that the Eucharist is a prayer that God will gather 'people of every race, language, and way of life to share in the one eternal banquet'.[31]

Pope John Paul called on priests and the whole community to show loving concern for those who are in a second union after the break-up of a marriage and cannot, therefore, receive Holy Communion: 'to make sure that they do not consider themselves as separated from the Church, for as baptised persons they can, and indeed must, share in her life. They should be encouraged to listen to the Word of God, to attend the Sacrifice of the Mass, to persevere in prayer, to contribute to works of charity and to community efforts in favour of justice, to bring up their children in the Christian faith, to cultivate the spirit and the practice of penance and thus implore, day by day, God's grace.'[32]

If we are to reach out to those who have drifted away from Sunday Mass, or who rarely attend, we need honestly to ask ourselves how welcoming our congregation is, how our community

---

27. Marty Haugen, 'All Are Welcome' (hymn).
28. Benedict XVI, *Sacramentum caritatis*, 83.
29. Cf. 1 Cor 11:20, 21.
30. *Novo millennio ineunte*, 50.
31. Eucharistic Prayer for Reconciliation II.
32. John Paul II, *Familiaris consortio*, 84.

would appear to someone who had not been there for some time, or who is coming for the first time.

If there are those who know that it would not be honest for them to receive the Eucharist because their way of life, in the area of justice, charity, chastity or other moral obligation, is seriously sinful and in fundamental conflict with the message of the Gospel, they should be able to recognise a community 'which by charity, by example and by prayer labours for their conversion'.[33]

How do young people perceive our Sunday celebrations? What part do they have in preparing the ceremony, in reading or singing? Do the Prayers of the Faithful express their concerns and hopes in language they can relate to? Do they see a celebration which is at the heart of the lives of those taking part, with people taking part as readers, singers, musicians and collectors, in which the whole congregation is actively participating? Do they sense anything of the amazement of a community in the presence of the death and resurrection of Christ?

Most of all, we need to grow in appreciation of what it means to say that the celebration of the Sunday Eucharist is the summit and source of the whole life of the parish and of every Christian community. What we do there is not just about some parts of our life. The whole Church is priestly because the whole Church offers the whole of itself along with the offering of Christ.[34] The priest prays at the Presentation of the Gifts that the Lord God will receive us and be pleased with the sacrifice we offer. This is the universal priesthood of every baptised Christian.

> Baptismal life, thus translated into relationships of mutual love and service, is in fact the life of 'the holy priestly community', of the 'spiritual house' [cf. 1 Pet 2:5] where spiritual sacrifices pleasing to God through Jesus Christ are offered [...] these sacrifices are not primarily liturgical cultic

---

33. *Lumen gentium*, 11.
34. See *Catechism of the Catholic Church*, 1546.

actions but the existential acts of the holy life of this community.[35]

To say that the Eucharist is the summit and the source is also to say that we need to open our minds and hearts to grasp that truth. Jesus said: 'Whoever comes to me will never be hungry, and whoever believes in me will never be thirsty' (Jn 6:35; NRSV). But the Book of Sirach seems to say the contrary: 'Those who eat me will hunger for more; those who drink me will thirst for more' (Sir 24:21).

Those words say something which is also true of the Eucharist. It is a truth which is particularly important in our world. The Eucharist is the presence of our future, the presence of the Goal of human life. At the same time it heightens our desire to share finally with the Risen Lord.

We are part of the affluent world, though it does not feel like it, especially when we contemplate the debts left to us by certain banks and by the way we 'lost the run of ourselves'. We are people whose need is not so much to be freed from hunger as to feel the hunger which only God can satisfy. We need to feel the restlessness and the incompleteness which modern living often seeks to silence. We need to hunger for more and to thirst for more than consumerism and materialism have to offer. We need to understand the Eucharist not only as the Living Bread which satisfies but as the Bread that makes us hunger for more.

There are two areas in particular where that hunger needs to be felt and unless *both* are experienced the real nature of human hunger is distorted.

Restless Until We Rest in God[36]
In the first place, the Eucharist arouses a hunger for the *absolute*. It is a sign of the ultimately unsatisfying nature of the nourishment that this life offers. Life is unsatisfying, not because it is evil, but

---

35. *Flesh of the Church, Flesh of Christ*, pp. 22, 23.
36. See Augustine, *Confessions*, i.1.

because it is good. It is good, but it is impermanent – nothing lasts for ever. It is good but it is vulnerable – everything is threatened by death, illness, our own sinfulness and the sinfulness of others. It is good but it is imperfect – even the most generous love is marred by selfishness; even the most noble cause can be perverted.

Distortions begin to happen when we become so absorbed in seeking good things that we blind ourselves to the fact that even the best things cannot satisfy the unlimited aspirations that are within us:

> In this creative restlessness beats and pulsates what is most deeply human – the search for truth, the insatiable need for the good, hunger for freedom, longing for the beautiful and the voice of conscience.[37]

The Eucharist is our contact with Christ, the first born of the new creation. In that new creation, we will find a goodness which is permanent, unthreatened, perfect: a goodness which can satisfy our hunger.

And that goodness will not be something alien or inhuman. It will be the solidarity, freedom, dignity and achievements of human history, 'cleansed this time from the stain of sin, illuminated and transfigured'.[38]

The Eucharist is, therefore, a sign of the inability of even the greatest human goods to satisfy us, because it is the presence of the One who is the fulfilment of all aspirations. We are created and redeemed for something greater than the world can offer and our hearts are restless until they rest in God.

The Eucharist, at the same time, far from turning us away from what is good in human life, is a sign and promise of the fact that all that is good in our lives and relationships is called to live for ever, transformed and perfected, vindicated and flourishing. We

---

37. *Redemptor hominis*, 18.
38. *Gaudium et spes*, 39.

are called to pass from death to life in Christ. The process of drawing humanity into that endless life has begun. That is what we celebrate, that is what is present, in the Eucharist.

The hunger which is celebrated in the Eucharist is not confined to certain areas of life, to holy times and holy places. It concerns every nook and cranny, every relationship, every decision, every achievement.

Within every person, at every moment and in every situation there is a hunger which can only be satisfied by being with Christ, risen from the dead, in the life he now lives with his Father. The real challenge in bringing the Gospel to bear on this world and the fundamental tragedy of our times is that this hunger is so often suppressed, so often unrecognised, so often dismissed.

Whatever the appearances, 'it is impossible to eradicate completely the sense of God'.[39] But that sense can be pushed almost completely beyond the horizon of people's concerns.

The unease, the restlessness, the powerlessness and the quiet desperation of much of modern life cannot be ignored. But the real meaning of these feelings can be and often is suppressed. The real meaning which the Christian Gospel shows us is that this restlessness and unease are 'the groans that cannot be put into words [...] the prayers that the Spirit makes for God's holy people' (Rom 8:26, 27; *New Jerusalem Bible*). In that light, instead of being a recipe for hopelessness and disillusionment, human restlessness becomes a sign of the greatness of our hope, reaching out to a destiny that eye has neither seen nor ear heard.

There is the core of the challenge that faces us: how to awaken and keep alive a sense of this hope which is too big for a matter-of-fact world to grasp. It was summed up in a phrase that stuck in my mind some years ago when somebody used it at a conference on secularisation: we need, he said, to find a way to 'evangelise people's desires'. We need to find a language and a way of life which will reveal the joy and the human richness of Christ's

---

39. *Reconciliatio et paenitentia*, 18.

promise, which is what we seek in all our longings, though we rarely recognise it.

We do not need to suppress our hopes and damp down our desires in the cynicism which believes that 'if something can go wrong, it will' and 'blessed is he who expects nothing for he shall not be disappointed'. We need rather to open our minds to the realisation that we are made for something greater, that the trouble with our hopes is not that they are too big but that they are too small. We really begin to understand our hopes and longings when we begin 'to grasp the breadth and the length, the height and the depth, so that, knowing the love of Christ which is beyond knowledge, [we] may be filled with the utter fullness of God' (Eph 3:18).

In other words, we need to be stretched in order to receive the fullness of God. St Augustine puts it like this:

> Suppose you want to fill some sort of bag [...] You know how big the object is that you want to put in and you see that the bag is narrow so you increase its capacity by stretching it. In the same way by delaying the fulfilment of desire God stretches it, by making us desire he expands the soul, and by this expansion he increases its capacity [...] That one syllable [God] contains all that we hope for [...] Let us stretch ourselves out towards him so that when he comes he may fill us.[40]

The Eucharist is at the very centre of the real world. It is the Reality which alone gives meaning to the chaos of human lives and human history. It is not a lay-by; it is the Road. Anything which does not in some way share in the truth made present in the Eucharist is at best a lay-by and at worst a road that carries one away from the destination.

The mythology of consumerism promises wealth and prestige, comfort, fitness, success. But it is a mythology that blinds. As

---

40. Augustine, Homily on the First Letter of John, Office of Readings, Friday Week 6.

Rolheiser puts it: 'When we stand before reality self-preoccupied, we will see precious little of what is actually there to be seen. Moreover, even what we do see will be distorted and shaped by self-interest [...] Our sense of reality shrinks accordingly.'[41]

That is why reflection on the Eucharist is a good test. The temptation is to get on with the 'bits' of the Gospel that 'work'. We can speak of good neighbourliness and decent moral standards, and people may well find that helpful, but these can easily coexist with attitudes that shrink our sense of reality. They have their own value and may be a way of opening a person up to the Good News, but we must be clear: evangelisation, properly speaking, is about awakening and addressing the hunger for absolute fulfilment; it is about the hunger which only God can satisfy.

The antidote to secularism will not be found in condemnations or in coercion. It will be found by allowing people to see a Truth which is richer, more satisfying, more liberating, more human, more worthy of our wholehearted commitment and effort than anything else. Hunger for that truth is what can be awakened and deepened by the Eucharist – they who eat him will hunger for more.

The difference that would become visible in a community where people were inspired and stretched and invigorated by that vision would be enormous. The Eucharist shows us a hope which gives a new dimension to human dignity and a new foundation for hope. When we look at ourselves in the light of our redemption in Christ, as Pope John Paul put it in his first encyclical, we are filled with deep amazement at human worth and dignity.[42]

'As long as you did it to one of the least of these'
The second aspect of the hunger which the Eucharist arouses in us is a hunger for justice. The Eucharist celebrates what humanity is called to be in Jesus Christ. The unlimited self-giving of the Lord

---

41. Ronald Rolheiser, *The Shattered Lantern* (London: Hodder and Stoughton, 1994), p. 27.
42. *Redemptor hominis*, 10.

in his broken Body and his flowing Blood is the standard for our treatment of one another. It also celebrates our faith that this unlimited love is given to all of us together. We are co-heirs with Christ, sharing his sufferings in order to share his glory (cf. Rom 8:17). God wishes all human beings to be saved and to come to the truth (cf. 1 Tim 2:3, 4).

The Eucharist makes present the Body of Christ. At the same time it builds up the Body of Christ which we are. Communion with the Body of Christ in the Eucharist signifies and brings about, or builds up, the intimate union of the faithful in the Body of Christ which is the Church.[43]

Celebration of the Eucharist commits us to believing in the peace and unity of God's kingdom and to recognising that our own sharing in that peace and unity is dependent on how we treat the sons and daughters of God.

By celebrating the Eucharist, we are expressing our readiness to enter the fulfilment of all our hopes, the eternal banquet. We are expressing our readiness to share with all of those who 'will come from east and west and sit down with Abraham and Isaac and Jacob at the feast in the kingdom of Heaven' (Mt 8:11).

But that is too comfortable a way of putting it. We are expressing the hope that we will be found worthy to sit at the feast. Put it another way: it is not just a matter of whether we are ready to share with people of other social conditions, times, places, races, beliefs and so on; it is a matter of whether they will be ready to share with us.

The union with God for which we hope is a union which can be entered only by those who can be recognised as brothers and sisters, those who have served Christ in the least of his brothers and sisters and who will be welcomed by Christ *in their name*: 'If you did it to them, you did it to me.' If there are those who have good reason to think that I am not a brother to them, then the Eucharist is a judgement on me.

---

43. Message of the Synod of Bishops, 1985.

That was the instruction of Christ, an instruction that the Church has always thought of in relation to the Eucharist — if you remember that your brother has something against you, go first and be reconciled before approaching the altar (cf. Mt 5:23f).

The justice to which the Eucharist points is the divine justice which exceeds anything we can imagine. One cannot ultimately make sense of human life if life is meaningless for any human being. Yet down the centuries thousands, millions, of people lived short, oppressed, miserable lives. Those people are beyond our help. That is another reason why the hope which God offers, and it alone, can bring a meaning which is big enough to free us from helplessness and absurdity. He offers dignity and eternal vindication to those who suffered in all the generations. It is:

> [...] a finally perfect justice for the living and the dead, for people of all times and places, a justice which Jesus Christ, installed as supreme Judge, will establish.[44]

The Eucharist challenges us, asking us whether we really believe in the peace and unity of God's kingdom. We proclaim that we are waiting for it in joyful hope. We claim, in other words, in every Mass, that we hunger for the coming of the kingdom.

Work for justice is a consequence of the promise we have received and celebrated in the Eucharist. We have been touched by the new creation of perfect justice and we have been challenged to live for it:

> The Congress has taught you to live the breaking of bread as Church, according to all its demands: welcoming, exchanging, sharing, going beyond barriers, being concerned for the conversion of people, the renunciation of prejudices, the transforming of our social milieu in structures and in spirit. You have understood that to be true and logical your

---

44. *Christian Freedom and Liberation*, 60.

meeting at the Eucharistic table must have practical consequences.[45]

Young people repeatedly tell us that attendance at Mass does not seem to produce the kind of change in attitudes and lifestyle that it should. No doubt the struggle to be just and open minded is more difficult than they realise; no doubt many of those who are at Mass are trying more sincerely than they are given credit for, and yet ... It is not a criticism to be easily dismissed, and certainly not when it is made about us who are called to celebrate the Eucharist as priests. The Mass, Karl Rahner reminded us, is necessarily the source of or the judgement on our love of neighbour, 'the very thing in which our priestly mission consists'.[46]

Do we feel entirely comfortable about our attitude to people who have, we feel, offended us? What is our attitude to people whose political, cultural, religious views we find particularly disagreeable? Are there people we would be a little apprehensive to see awaiting us at the throne of God?

Do we feel a genuine outrage at the suffering of people in the Third World? At the heavenly banquet, how can we face the victims of African famine, babies who died for want of a mixture worth a couple of pence to counteract the effects of diarrhoea, victims of floods and earthquakes; people whose children have been denied basic education and whose grandchildren will, in all likelihood, be denied it too? Do we imagine that those who are innocent victims of violence through crime or war or terrorism would be easily persuaded that we have done all that they might have expected a brother or sister to do? Do we look on their situation with anything like the sense of urgency that they have a right to expect?

The fact that we can see no immediate solution to these sufferings makes them not one whit less intolerable, especially for

---

45. John Paul II, Message to Eucharistic Congress, Lourdes, 1981.
46. Karl Rahner, *Meditations on Priestly Life* (London: Sheed and Ward, 1973), p. 213.

us who hope that these brothers and sisters will welcome us to the eternal banquet.

The Eucharist, properly understood, demands that we look critically at our own lifestyle, at the waste that passes for normal in our societies and in our own lives. We are faced with a crisis with regard to the exploitation of the resources of the earth, a crisis which is a moral challenge:

> Simplicity, moderation and discipline, as well as a spirit of sacrifice, must become part of everyday life.[47]

That sense of outrage at injustice should not express itself through the easy option of constantly berating the evils of whatever people or groups one thinks are responsible. The balance is something that is reflected by the approach of Mary at Cana. Faced with an obvious example of bad planning, of irresponsibility, of people utterly failing to help themselves, she does not engage in moralising or condemnation. She does not take refuge in the easy superiority of 'Let that be a lesson to you!' Nor does she escape into impotent regret: 'It's too late now.' Nor resort to buck-passing: 'There must be somebody whose job it is to help these poor people; let them do something about it.' She just sees people in need. Even though there seemed to be little that could be done, she took what steps she could to try to improve the situation. The step she did take seemed to be quite inadequate to resolve the problem but she took it anyway. The dominant attitude she showed was one of real compassion and feeling for people in trouble and a practical consideration of what could be done.

The same approach has been part of the approach of the Legion of Mary to apparently insoluble problems:

> No matter what may be the degree of the difficulty, a step must be taken. Of course, the step should be as effective as it

---

47. John Paul II, Message for the World Day of Peace, 1990.

can be. But if an effective step is not in view, then we must take a less effective one. And if the latter is not available, then some active gesture (that is not merely a prayer) must be made which, though of no apparent practical value, at least tends towards or has some relation to the objective. This final challenging gesture is what the Legion has been calling 'Symbolic Action'.[48]

However large and daunting the problem, we should offer our five loaves and two fish.

Hunger for God
God our Father
source of all joy in heaven and on earth,
you have prepared for us a banquet of unending joy.
There you will remove the mourning veil
covering all peoples,
wipe away the tears from every cheek
and bring us into absolute joy
in your peace which passes all understanding.

May we see more clearly
that the meaning of our lives
is to *be* a hunger, a thirst,
an insatiable longing for you.

May our celebration of the Eucharist
increase our awareness of the hunger
which is the deepest truth of our being,
and may it *be* for us the pledge of eternal life
in which our hunger is satisfied.

---

48. From the Official Handbook of the Legion of Mary, Dublin, 1993, pp. 286–7.

May we recognise in every human being
a brother or sister,
called to share with us
in the joy and glory of Christ's risen Body –
the Body given up for us,
the Body which we receive,
the Body which we are,
the Body in which we make our prayer,
through Christ our Lord.
Amen.